SCIENTIFIC
AMERICAN™

CUTTING-EDGE SCIENCE™

The Future of
the Web

ROSEN
PUBLISHING®

New York

Published in 2007 by The Rosen Publishing Group, Inc.
29 East 21st Street, New York, NY 10010

The articles in this book first appeared in the pages of *Scientific American*,
as follows: "Filtering Information on the Internet" by Paul Resnick,
March 1997; "Preserving the Internet" by Brewster Kahle, March 1997;
"Searching the Internet" by Clifford Lynch, March 1997; "XML and the
Second-Generation Web" by Jon Bosak and Tim Bray, May 1999;
"Hypersearching the Web" by Members of the "Clever" Project, June
1999; "The Semantic Web" by Tim Berners-Lee, James Hendler and Ora
Lassila, May 2001; "The Worldwide Computer" by David P. Anderson
and John Kubiatowicz, March 2002.

First Edition

Library of Congress Cataloging-in-Publication Data

The future of the Web.
    p. cm.—(Scientific American cutting-edge science)
Includes index.
ISBN-13: 978-1-4042-0989-3
ISBN-10: 1-4042-0989-1 (library binding)
1. World Wide Web. 2. Internet. I. Scientific American.
TK5105.888.F87 2006
004.67'8—dc22

                           2006024288

Manufactured in the United States of America

On the cover: An artist's rendition of how information is transferred
between individual computers and the World Wide Web. Background:
An illustration of how computers are networked by the Internet.

Illustration credits: Cover, pp. 9, 21, 26, 29, 54, 56 Bryan Christie; p. 23
Bryan Christie/Source: Matthew K. Gray; pp. 38, 47 Laurie Grace; pp. 98,
100–101, 108 XPLANE.

Contents

Introduction

The dotcom bubble may have finally burst but there can be no doubt that the Internet has forever changed the way we communicate, do business and find information of all kinds. *Scientific American* has regularly covered the advances making this transformation possible. And during the past five years alone, many leading researchers and computer scientists have aired their views on the Web in our pages.

In this collection, expert authors discuss a range of topics—from XML and hypersearching the web to filtering information and preserving the Internet in one vast archive. Other articles cover more recent ideas, including ways to make Web content more meaningful to machines and plans to create an operating system that would span the Internet as a whole.

—The Editors

I. "Filtering Information on the Internet"

by Paul Resnick

Look for the labels to decide if unknown software and World Wide Web sites are safe and interesting

The Internet is often called a global village, suggesting a huge but close-knit community that shares common values and experiences. The metaphor is misleading. Many cultures coexist on the Internet and at times clash. In its public spaces, people interact commercially and socially with strangers as well as with acquaintances and friends. The city is a more apt metaphor, with its suggestion of unlimited opportunities and myriad dangers.

To steer clear of the most obviously offensive, dangerous or just boring neighborhoods, users can employ some mechanical filtering techniques that identify easily definable risks. One technique is to analyze the contents of on-line material. Thus, virus-detection software searches for code fragments that it knows are common in virus programs. Services such as AltaVista and Lycos can either highlight or exclude World Wide Web documents containing particular words. My colleagues and I have been at work on another filtering technique based on electronic labels that can be added to Web sites to describe digital works. These labels can convey characteristics that require human judgment—whether the Web page is funny or offensive—as well as information not readily apparent from the words and graphics, such as the Web site's policies about the use or resale of personal data.

The Massachusetts Institute of Technology's World Wide Web Consortium has developed a set of technical standards called PICS (Platform for Internet Content Selection) so that people can electronically distribute descriptions of digital works in a simple, computer-readable form. Computers can process these labels in the background, automatically shielding users from undesirable material or directing their attention to sites of particular interest. The original impetus for PICS was to allow parents and teachers to screen materials they felt were inappropriate for children using the Net. Rather than censoring what is distributed, as the Communications Decency Act and other legislative initiatives have tried to do, PICS enables users to control what they receive.

What's in a Label?

PICS labels can describe any aspect of a document or a Web site. The first labels identified items that might run afoul of local indecency laws. For example, the Recreational Software Advisory Council (RSAC) adapted its computer-game rating system for the Internet. Each RSACi (the "i" stands for "Internet") label has four numbers, indicating levels of violence, nudity, sex and potentially offensive language. Another organization, SafeSurf, has developed a vocabulary with nine separate scales. Labels can reflect other concerns beyond indecency, however. A privacy vocabulary, for example, could describe Web sites' information practices, such as what personal information they collect and whether they resell it. Similarly, an intellectual-property vocabulary could describe the conditions under which an item could be viewed or reproduced. And various Web-indexing organizations could develop labels that indicate the subject categories or the reliability of information from a site.

Labels could even help protect computers from exposure to viruses. It has become increasingly popular to download small fragments of computer code, bug fixes and even entire applications from Internet sites. People generally trust that the software they download will not introduce a virus; they could add a margin of safety by checking for labels that vouch for the software's safety. The vocabulary for such labels might indicate which virus checks have been run on the software or the level of confidence in the code's safety.

In the physical world, labels can be attached to the things they describe, or they can be distributed separately. For example, the new cars in an automobile showroom display stickers describing features and prices, but potential customers can also consult independent listings such as consumer-interest magazines. Similarly, PICS labels can be attached or detached. An information provider that wishes to offer descriptions of its own materials can directly embed labels in Web documents or send them along with items retrieved from the Web. Independent third parties can describe materials as well. For instance, the Simon Wiesenthal Center, which tracks the activities of neo-Nazi groups, could publish PICS labels that identify Web pages containing neo-Nazi propaganda. These labels would be stored on a separate server; not everyone who visits the neo-Nazi pages would see the Wiesenthal Center labels, but those who were interested could instruct their software to check automatically for the labels.

Software can be configured not merely to make its users aware of labels but to act on them directly. Several Web software packages, including CyberPatrol and Microsoft's Internet Explorer, already use the PICS standard to control users' access to sites. Such software can make its decisions based on any PICS-compatible vocabulary. A user who plugs in the RSACi vocabulary can set the maximum acceptable levels of language, nudity, sex and violence. A user who plugs in a software-safety vocabulary can decide precisely which virus checks are required.

In addition to blocking unwanted materials, label processing can assist in finding desirable materials. If a user expresses a preference for works of high literary quality, a search engine might be able to suggest links to items labeled that way. Or if the user prefers that personal data not be collected or sold, a Web server can offer a version of its service that does not depend on collecting personal information.

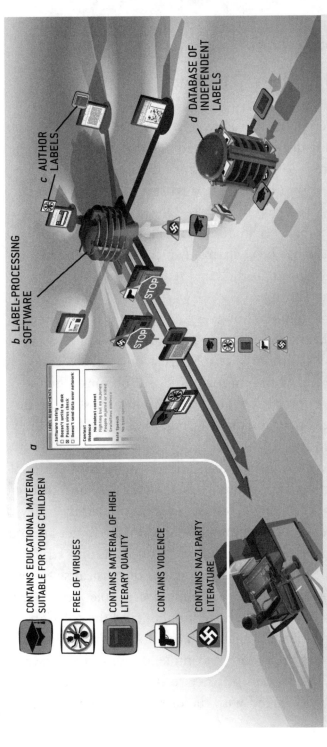

CONTAINS EDUCATIONAL MATERIAL SUITABLE FOR YOUNG CHILDREN

FREE OF VIRUSES

CONTAINS MATERIAL OF HIGH LITERARY QUALITY

CONTAINS VIOLENCE

CONTAINS NAZI PARTY LITERATURE

b LABEL-PROCESSING SOFTWARE

c AUTHOR LABELS

d DATABASE OF INDEPENDENT LABELS

a

LABEL REQUIREMENTS

Software safety
☐ Doesn't write to disk
☒ Passes virus check
☒ Doesn't send data over network

Content
Violence
○ No violent content
○ Fighting but no injuries
○ People injured or killed
○ Gratuitous violence

Hate Speech
○ No hate

FILTERING SYSTEM for the World Wide Web allows individuals to decide for themselves what they want to see. Users specify safety and content requirements (*a*), which label-processing software (*b*) then consults to determine whether to block access to certain pages (marked with a stop sign). Labels can be affixed by the Web site's author (*c*), or a rating agency can store its labels in a separate database (*d*).

9

Establishing Trust

Not every label is trustworthy. The creator of a virus can easily distribute a misleading label claiming that the software is safe. Checking for labels merely converts the question of whether to trust a piece of software to one of trusting the labels. One solution is to use cryptographic techniques that can determine whether a document has been changed since its label was created and to ensure that the label really is the work of its purported author.

That solution, however, simply changes the question again, from one of trusting a label to one of trusting the label's author. Alice may trust Bill's labels if she has worked with him for years or if he runs a major software company whose reputation is at stake. Or she might trust an auditing organization of some kind to vouch for Bill.

Of course, some labels address matters of personal taste rather than points of fact. Users may find themselves not trusting certain labels, simply because they disagree with the opinions behind them. To get around this problem, systems such as GroupLens and Firefly recommend books, articles, videos or musical selections based on the ratings of like-minded people. People rate items with which they are familiar, and the software compares those ratings with opinions registered by other users. In making recommendations, the software assigns the highest priority to items approved by people who agreed with the user's evaluations of other materials. People need not know who agreed with them; they can participate anonymously, preserving the privacy of their evaluations and reading habits.

Widespread reliance on labeling raises a number of social concerns. The most obvious are the questions of who decides how to label sites and what labels are acceptable. Ideally, anyone could label a site, and everyone could establish individual filtering rules. But there is a concern that authorities could assign labels to sites or dictate criteria for sites to label themselves. In an example from a different medium, the television industry, under pressure from the U.S. government, has begun to rate its shows for age appropriateness.

Mandatory self-labeling need not lead to censorship, so long as individuals can decide which labels to ignore. But people may not always have this power. Improved individual control removes one rationale for central control but does not prevent its imposition. Singapore and China, for instance, are experimenting with national "firewalls"—combinations of software and hardware that block their citizens' access to certain newsgroups and Web sites.

Another concern is that even without central censorship, any widely adopted vocabulary will encourage people to make lazy decisions that do not reflect their values. Today many parents who may not agree with the criteria used to assign movie ratings still forbid their children to see movies rated PG-13 or R; it is too hard for them to weigh the merits of each movie by themselves.

Labeling organizations must choose vocabularies carefully to match the criteria that most people care about, but even so, no single vocabulary can serve everyone's needs. Labels concerned only with rating the level of sexual content at a site will be of no use to someone concerned about hate speech. And no labeling system is a full substitute for a thorough and thoughtful evaluation: movie reviews in a newspaper can be far more enlightening than any set of predefined codes.

Perhaps most troubling is the suggestion that any labeling system, no matter how well conceived and executed, will tend to stifle noncommercial communication. Labeling requires human time and energy; many sites of limited interest will probably go unlabeled. Because of safety concerns, some people will block access to materials that are unlabeled or whose labels are untrusted. For such people, the Internet will function more like broadcasting, providing access only to sites with sufficient mass-market appeal to merit the cost of labeling.

While lamentable, this problem is an inherent one that is not caused by labeling. In any medium, people tend to avoid the unknown when there are risks involved, and it is far easier to get information about material that is of wide interest than about items that appeal to a small audience.

Although the Net nearly eliminates the technical barriers to communication with strangers, it does not remove the social costs. Labels can reduce those costs, by letting us control when we extend trust to potentially boring or dangerous software or Web sites. The challenge will be to let labels guide our exploration of the global city of the Internet and not limit our travels.

The Author

PAUL RESNICK joined AT&T Labs–Research in 1995 as the founding member of the Public Policy Research group. He is also chairman of the PICS working group of the World Wide Web Consortium. Resnick received his Ph.D. in computer science in 1992 from the Massachusetts Institute of Technology and was an assistant professor at the M.I.T. Sloan School of Management before moving to AT&T.

Further Reading

Rating the Net. Jonathan Weinberg in *Hastings Communications and Entertainment Law Journal*, Vol. 19; March 1997 (in press). Available on the World Wide Web at http://www. msen.com/ ~weinberg/rating.htm

Recommender Systems. Special section in *Communications of the ACM*, Vol. 40, No. 3; March 1997 (in press).

The Platform for Internet Content Selection home page is available on the World Wide Web at **http:// www.w3.org/PICS**

"Preserving the
2. Internet"

by Brewster Kahle

*An archive of the Internet may prove to be a vital
record for historians, businesses and governments*

Manuscripts from the library of Alexandria in
ancient Egypt disappeared in a fire. The early printed
books decayed into unrecognizable shreds. Many of
the oldest cinematic films were recycled for their silver
content. Unfortunately, history may repeat itself in the
evolution of the Internet—and its World Wide Web.

No one has tried to capture a comprehensive record
of the text and images contained in the documents
that appear on the Web. The history of print and film
is a story of loss and partial reconstruction. But this
scenario need not be repeated for the Web, which has
increasingly evolved into a storehouse of valuable
scientific, cultural and historical information.

The dropping costs of digital storage mean that a
permanent record of the Web and the rest of the
Internet can be preserved by a small group of technical
professionals equipped with a modest complement of
computer workstations and data storage devices. A year
ago I and a few others set out to realize this vision as
part of a venture known as the Internet Archive.

By the time this article is published, we will have
taken a snapshot of all parts of the Web freely and

technically accessible to us. This collection of data will measure perhaps as much as two trillion bytes (two terabytes) of data, ranging from text to video to audio recording. In comparison, the Library of Congress contains about 20 terabytes of text information. In the coming months, our computers and storage media will make records of other areas of the Internet, including the Gopher information system and the Usenet bulletin boards. The material gathered so far has already proved a useful resource to historians. In the future, it may provide the raw material for a carefully indexed, searchable library.

The logistics of taking a snapshot of the Web are relatively simple. Our Internet Archive operates with a staff of 10 people from offices located in a converted military base—the Presidio—in downtown San Francisco; it also runs an information-gathering computer in the San Diego Supercomputer Center at the University of California at San Diego.

The software on our computers "crawls" the Net—downloading documents, called pages, from one site after another. Once a page is captured, the software looks for cross references, or links, to other pages. It uses the Web's hyperlinks—addresses embedded within a document page—to move to other pages. The software then makes copies again and seeks additional links contained in the new pages. The crawler avoids downloading duplicate copies of pages by checking the identification names, called uniform resource locators (URLs), against a database. Programs such as Digital

Equipment Corporation's AltaVista also employ crawler software for indexing Web sites.

What makes this experiment possible is the dropping cost of data storage. The price of a gigabyte (a billion bytes) of hard-disk space is $200, whereas tape storage using an automated mounting device costs $20 a gigabyte. We chose hard-disk storage for a small amount of data that users of the archive are likely to access frequently and a robotic device that mounts and reads tapes automatically for less used information. A disk drive accesses data in an average of 15 milliseconds, whereas tapes require four minutes. Frequently accessed information might be historical documents or a set of URLs no longer in use.

We plan to update the information gathered at least every few months. The first full record required nearly a year to compile. In future passes through the Web, we will be able to update only the information that has changed since our last perusal.

The text, graphics, audio clips and other data collected from the Web will never be comprehensive, because the crawler software cannot gain access to many of the hundreds of thousands of sites. Publishers restrict access to data or store documents in a format inaccessible to simple crawler programs. Still, the archive gives a feel of what the Web looks like during a given period of time even though it does not constitute a full record.

After gathering and storing the public contents of the Internet, what services will the archive provide? We possess the capability of supplying documents that are no longer available from the original publisher, an important function if the Web's hypertext system is to become a medium for scholarly publishing. Such a service could also prove worthwhile for business research. And the archival data might serve as a "copy of record" for the government or other institutions with publicly available documents. So, over time, the archive would come to resemble a digital library.

Keeping Missing Links

Historians have already found the material useful. David Allison of the Smithsonian Institution has tapped into the archive for a presidential election Web site exhibit at the museum, a project he compares to saving videotapes of early television campaign advertisements. Many of the links for these Web sites, such as those for Texas Senator Phil Gramm's campaign, have already disappeared from the Internet.

Creating an archive touches on an array of issues, from privacy to copyright. What if a college student created a Web page that had pictures of her then current boyfriend? What if she later wanted to "tear them up," so to speak, yet they lived on in the archive? Should she have the right to remove them? In contrast, should a public figure—a U.S. senator, for instance—be able to erase data posted from his or her college years? Does collecting information made available to the public violate the "fair use" provisions of the copyright law? The issues are not easily resolved.

To address these worries, we let authors exclude their works from the archive. We are also considering allowing researchers to obtain broad censuses of the archive data instead of individual documents—one could count the total number of references to pachyderms on the Web, for instance, but not look at a specific elephant home page. These measures, we hope, will suffice to allay immediate concerns about privacy and intellectual-property rights. Over time, the issues addressed in setting up the Internet Archive might help resolve the larger policy debates on intellectual property and privacy by testing concepts such as fair use on the Internet.

The Internet Archive complements other projects intended to ensure the longevity of information on the Internet. The Commission on Preservation and Access in Washington, D.C., researches how to ensure that data are not lost as the standard formats for digital storage media change over the years. In another effort, the Internet Engineering Task Force and other groups have labored on technical standards that give a unique identification name to digital documents. These uniform resource names (URNs), as they are called, could supplement the URLs that currently access Web documents. Giving a document a URN attempts to ensure that it can be traced after a link disappears, because estimates put the average lifetime for a URL at 44 days. The URN would be able to locate other URLs that still provided access to the desired documents.

Other, more limited attempts to archive parts of the Internet have also begun. DejaNews keeps a record of messages on the Usenet bulletin boards, and InReference archives Internet mailing lists. Both support themselves with revenue from advertisers, a possible funding source for the Internet Archive as well. Until now, I have funded the project with money I received from the sale of an Internet software and services company. Major computer companies have also donated equipment.

It will take many years before an infrastructure that assures Internet preservation becomes well established— and for questions involving intellectual-property issues to resolve themselves. For our part, we feel that it is important to proceed with the collection of the archival material because it can never be recovered in the future. And the opportunity to capture a record of the birth of a new medium will then be lost.

The Author

BREWSTER KAHLE founded the Internet Archive in April 1996. He invented the Wide Area Information Servers (WAIS) system in 1989 and started a company, WAIS, Inc., in 1992 to commercialize this Internet publishing software. The company helped to bring commercial and government agencies onto the Internet by selling publishing tools and production services. Kahle also served as a principal designer of the Connection Machine, a supercomputer produced by Thinking Machines. He received a bachelor's degree from the Massachusetts Institute of Technology in 1982.

"Searching the 3. Internet"

by Clifford Lynch

*Combining the skills of the librarian and the computer
scientist may help organize the anarchy of the Internet*

One sometimes hears the Internet characterized as
the world's library for the digital age. This description
does not stand up under even casual examination. The
Internet—and particularly its collection of multimedia
resources known as the World Wide Web—was not
designed to support the organized publication and
retrieval of information, as libraries are. It has evolved
into what might be thought of as a chaotic repository
for the collective output of the world's digital "printing
presses." This storehouse of information contains not
only books and papers but raw scientific data, menus,
meeting minutes, advertisements, video and audio
recordings, and transcripts of interactive conversations.
The ephemeral mixes everywhere with works of lasting
importance.

In short, the Net is not a digital library. But if it is
to continue to grow and thrive as a new means of
communication, something very much like traditional
library services will be needed to organize, access and
preserve networked information. Even then, the Net will
not resemble a traditional library, because its contents
are more widely dispersed than a standard collection.

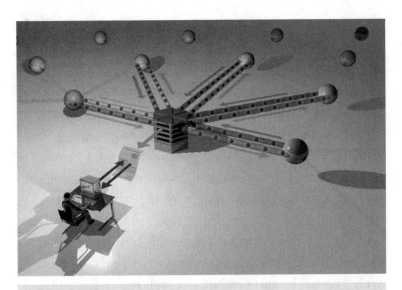

SEARCH ENGINE operates by visiting, or "crawling" through, World Wide Web sites, pictured as globes. The lines represent the output from and input to the engine's server (*tower at center*), where Web pages are downloaded. Software on the server computes an index (*page*) that can be accessed by users.

Consequently, the librarian's classification and selection skills must be complemented by the computer scientist's ability to automate the task of indexing and storing information. Only a synthesis of the differing perspectives brought by both professions will allow this new medium to remain viable.

At the moment, computer technology bears most of the responsibility for organizing information on the Internet. In theory, software that automatically classifies and indexes collections of digital data can address the glut of information on the Net—and the inability of human indexers and bibliographers to cope with it.

Automating information access has the advantage of directly exploiting the rapidly dropping costs of computers and avoiding the high expense and delays of human indexing.

But, as anyone who has ever sought information on the Web knows, these automated tools categorize information differently than people do. In one sense, the job performed by the various indexing and cataloguing tools known as search engines is highly democratic. Machine-based approaches provide uniform and equal access to all the information on the Net. In practice, this electronic egalitarianism can prove a mixed blessing. Web "surfers" who type in a search request are often overwhelmed by thousands of responses. The search results frequently contain references to irrelevant Web sites while leaving out others that hold important material.

Crawling the Web

The nature of electronic indexing can be understood by examining the way Web search engines, such as Lycos or Digital Equipment Corporation's AltaVista, construct indexes and find information requested by a user. Periodically, they dispatch programs (sometimes referred to as Web crawlers, spiders or indexing robots) to every site they can identify on the Web—each site being a set of documents, called pages, that can be accessed over the network. The Web crawlers download and then examine these pages and extract indexing information that can be used to describe them. This process—details of which vary among search engines— may include simply locating most of the words that appear in Web pages or performing sophisticated analyses to identify key words and phrases. These data are then stored in the search engine's database, along with an address, termed a uniform resource locator (URL), that represents where the file resides. A user then deploys a browser, such as the familiar Netscape,

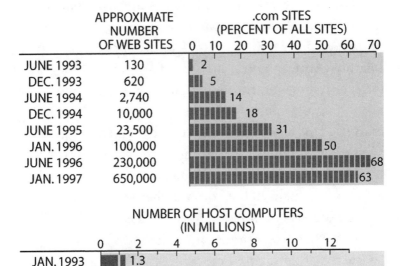

	APPROXIMATE NUMBER OF WEB SITES	.com SITES (PERCENT OF ALL SITES)
JUNE 1993	130	2
DEC. 1993	620	5
JUNE 1994	2,740	14
DEC. 1994	10,000	18
JUNE 1995	23,500	31
JAN. 1996	100,000	50
JUNE 1996	230,000	68
JAN. 1997	650,000	63

NUMBER OF HOST COMPUTERS
(IN MILLIONS)

JAN. 1993	1.3
JAN. 1994	2.2
JAN. 1995	4.9
JAN. 1996	9.5
JULY 1996	12.9

GROWTH AND CHANGE on the Internet are reflected in the burgeoning number of Web sites, host computers and commercial, or ".com," sites.

to submit queries to the search engine's database. The query produces a list of Web resources, the URLs that can be clicked on to connect to the sites identified by the search.

Existing search engines service millions of queries a day. Yet it has become clear that they are less than ideal for retrieving an ever growing body of information on the Web. In contrast to human indexers, automated programs have difficulty identifying characteristics of a document such as its overall theme or its genre—whether it is a poem or a play, or even an advertisement.

The Web, moreover, still lacks standards that would facilitate automated indexing. As a result, documents on the Web are not structured so that programs can reliably extract the routine information that a human indexer might find through a cursory inspection: author, date of publication, length of text and subject matter. (This information is known as metadata.) A Web crawler might turn up the desired article authored by Jane Doe. But it might also find thousands of other articles in which such a common name is mentioned in the text or in a bibliographic reference.

Publishers sometimes abuse the indiscriminate character of automated indexing. A Web site can bias the selection process to attract attention to itself by repeating within a document a word, such as "sex," that is known to be queried often. The reason: a search engine will display first the URLs for the documents that mention a search term most frequently. In contrast, humans can easily see around simpleminded tricks.

The professional indexer can describe the components of individual pages of all sorts (from text to video) and can clarify how those parts fit together into a database of information. Civil War photographs, for example, might form part of a collection that also includes period music and soldier diaries. A human indexer can describe a site's rules for the collection and retention of programs in, say, an archive that stores Macintosh software. Analyses of a site's purpose, history and policies are beyond the capabilities of a crawler program.

Another drawback of automated indexing is that most search engines recognize text only. The intense interest in the Web, though, has come about because of the medium's ability to display images, whether graphics or video clips. Some research has moved forward toward finding colors or patterns within images. But no program can deduce the underlying meaning and cultural significance of an image (for example, that a group of men dining represents the Last Supper).

At the same time, the way information is structured on the Web is changing so that it often cannot be examined by Web crawlers. Many Web pages are no longer static files that can be analyzed and indexed by such programs. In many cases, the information displayed in a document is computed by the Web site during a search in response to the user's request. The site might assemble a map, a table and a text document from different areas of its database, a disparate collection of information that conforms to the user's query. A newspaper's Web site, for instance, might allow a reader to specify that only stories on the oil-equipment business be displayed in a personalized version of the paper. The database of stories from which this document is put together could not be searched by a Web crawler that visits the site.

A growing body of research has attempted to address some of the problems involved with automated classification methods. One approach seeks to attach metadata to files so that indexing systems can collect

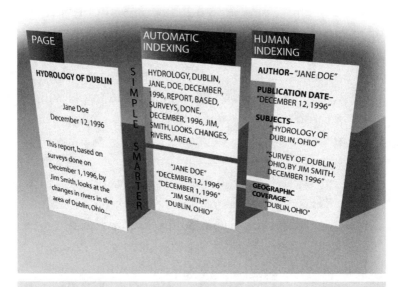

AUTOMATED INDEXING, used by Web crawler software, analyzes a page (*left panel*) by designating most words as indexing terms (*top center*) or by grouping words into simple phrases (*bottom center*). Human indexing (*right*) gives additional context about the subject of a page.

this information. The most advanced effort is the Dublin Core Metadata program and an affiliated endeavor, the Warwick Framework—the first named after a workshop in Dublin, Ohio, the other for a colloquy in Warwick, England. The workshops have defined a set of metadata elements that are simpler than those in traditional library cataloguing and have also created methods for incorporating them within pages on the Web.

Categorization of metadata might range from title or author to type of document (text or video, for instance). Either automated indexing software or humans may derive the metadata, which can then be attached to a Web page for retrieval by a crawler. Precise and detailed human annotations can provide a more in-depth characterization of a page than can an automated indexing program alone.

Where costs can be justified, human indexers have begun the laborious task of compiling bibliographies of some Web sites. The Yahoo database, a commercial venture, classifies sites by broad subject area. And a research project at the University of Michigan is one of several efforts to develop more formal descriptions of sites that contain material of scholarly interest.

Not Just a Library

The extent to which either human classification skills or automated indexing and searching strategies are needed will depend on the people who use the Internet and on the business prospects for publishers. For many communities of scholars, the model of an organized collection—a digital library—still remains relevant. For other groups, an uncontrolled, democratic medium may provide the best vehicle for information dissemination. Some users, from financial analysts to spies, want comprehensive access to raw databases of information, free of any controls or editing. For them, standard search engines provide real benefits because they forgo any selective filtering of data.

The diversity of materials on the Net goes far beyond the scope of the traditional library. A library does not provide quality rankings of the works in a collection. Because of the greater volume of networked information, Net users want guidance about where to spend the limited amount of time they have to research a subject. They may need to know the three "best" documents for a given purpose. They want this information without paying the costs of employing humans to critique the myriad Web sites. One solution that again calls for human involvement is to share judgments about what is worthwhile. Software-based rating systems have begun to let users describe the quality of particular Web sites.

Software tools search the Internet and also separate the good from the bad. New programs may be needed, though, to ease the burden of feeding the crawlers that repeatedly scan Web sites. Some Web site managers have reported that their computers are spending enormous amounts of time in providing crawlers with information to index, instead of servicing the people they hope to attract with their offerings.

To address this issue, Mike Schwartz and his colleagues at the University of Colorado at Boulder developed software, called Harvest, that lets a Web site compile indexing data for the pages it holds and to ship the information on request to the Web sites for the various search engines. In so doing, Harvest's automated indexing program, or gatherer, can avoid having a Web crawler export the entire contents of a given site across the network.

Crawler programs bring a copy of each page back to their home sites to extract the terms that make up an

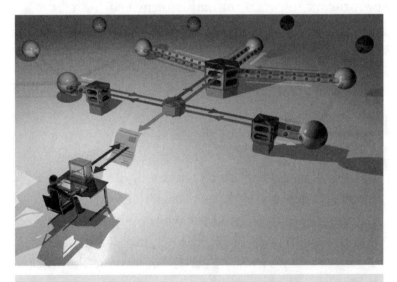

HARVEST, a new search-engine architecture, would derive indexing terms using software called gatherers that reside at Web sites (*boxes near globes*) or operate in a central computer (*hexagon*). By so doing, the search engine can avoid downloading all the documents from a Web site, an activity that burdens network traffic. The search engine's server (*structure at center*) would simply ask the gatherers (*dark arrows*) for a file of key words (*light arrows*) that could be processed into an index (*page*) for querying by a user.

index, a process that consumes a great deal of network capacity (bandwidth). The gatherer, instead, sends only a file of indexing terms. Moreover, it exports only information about those pages that have been altered since they were last accessed, thus alleviating the load on the network and the computers tied to it.

Gatherers might also serve a different function. They may give publishers a framework to restrict the information that gets exported from their Web sites. This degree of control is needed because the Web has begun to evolve beyond a distribution medium for free information. Increasingly, it facilitates access to proprietary information that is furnished for a fee. This material may not be open for the perusal of Web crawlers. Gatherers, though, could distribute only the information that publishers wish to make available, such as links to summaries or samples of the information stored at a site.

As the Net matures, the decision to opt for a given information collection method will depend mostly on users. For which users will it then come to resemble a library, with a structured approach to building collections? And for whom will it remain anarchic, with access supplied by automated systems?

Users willing to pay a fee to underwrite the work of authors, publishers, indexers and reviewers can sustain the tradition of the library. In cases where information is furnished without charge or is advertiser supported, low-cost computer-based indexing will most likely dominate—the same unstructured environment that characterizes much of the contemporary Internet. Thus, social and economic issues, rather than techno-logical ones, will exert the greatest influence in shaping the future of information retrieval on the Internet.

The Author

CLIFFORD LYNCH is director of library automation at the University of California's Office of the President, where he oversees MELVYL, one of the largest public-access information retrieval systems. Lynch, who received a doctorate in computer science from the University of California, Berkeley, also teaches at Berkeley's School of Information Management and Systems. He is a past president of the American Society for Information Science and a fellow of the American Association for the Advancement of Science. He leads the Architectures and Standards Working Group for the Coalition for Network Information.

"Finding Pictures on the Web"

by Gary Stix, *staff writer*

The Internet came into its own a few years ago, when the World Wide Web arrived with its dazzling array of photography, animation, graphics, sound and video that ranged in subject matter from high art to the patently lewd. Despite the multimedia barrage, finding things on the hundreds of thousands of Web sites still mostly requires searching indexes for words and numbers.

Someone who types the words "French flag" into the popular search engine AltaVista might retrieve the requested graphic, as long as it were captioned by those two identifying words. But what if someone could visualize a blue, white and red banner but did not know its country of origin?

Ideally, a search engine should allow the user to draw or scan in a rectangle with vertical thirds that are colored blue, white and red—and then find any matching images stored on myriad Web sites. In the past few years, techniques that combine key-word indexing with image analysis have begun to pave the way for the first image search engines.

Although these prototypes suggest possibilities for the indexing of visual information, they also demonstrate the crudeness of existing tools and the continuing reliance on text to track down imagery. One project, called WebSEEk, based at Columbia University, illustrates the workings of an image search engine. WebSEEk begins by downloading files found by trolling the Web. It then attempts to locate file names containing acronyms, such as GIF or MPEG, that designate graphics or video content. It also looks for words in the names that might identify the subject of the files. When the software finds an image, it analyzes the prevalence of different colors and where they are located. Using this information, it can distinguish among photographs, graphics and black-and-white or gray images. The software also compresses each picture so that it can be represented as an icon, a miniature image for display alongside other icons. For a video, it will extract key frames from different scenes.

A user begins a search by selecting a category from a menu—"cats," for example. WebSEEk provides a sampling of icons for the "cats" category. To narrow the search, the user can click on any icons that show black cats. Using its previously generated color analysis, the search engine looks for matches of images that have a similar color profile. The presentation of the next set of icons may show black cats—but also some marmalade cats sitting on black cushions. A visitor to WebSEEk can refine a search by adding or excluding certain colors from an image when initiating subsequent queries. Leaving out yellows or oranges might get rid of the odd marmalade. More simply, when presented with a series of icons, the user can also specify those images that do not contain black cats in order to guide the program away from mistaken choices. So far WebSEEk has downloaded and indexed more than 650,000 pictures from tens of thousands of Web sites.

Other image-searching projects include efforts at the University of Chicago, the University of California at San Diego, Carnegie Mellon University, the Massachusetts Institute of Technology's Media Lab and the University of California at Berkeley. A number of commercial companies, including IBM and Virage, have crafted software that can be used for searching corporate networks or databases. And two companies—Excalibur Technologies and Interpix Software—have collaborated to supply software to the Web-based indexing concerns Yahoo and Infoseek.

One of the oldest image searchers, IBM's Query by Image Content (QBIC), produces more sophisticated matching of image features than, say, WebSEEk can. It is able not only to pick out the colors in an image but also to gauge texture by several measures—contrast (the black and white of zebra stripes), coarseness (stones versus pebbles) and directionality (linear fence posts versus omnidirectional flower petals). QBIC also has a limited ability to search for shapes within an image. Specifying a pink dot on a green background turns up flowers and other photographs with similar shapes and colors, as shown above. Possible applications range from the selection of wallpaper patterns to enabling police to identify gang members by clothing type.

All these programs do nothing more than match one visual feature with another. They still require a human observer—or accompanying text—to confirm whether an object is a cat or a cushion. For more than a decade, the artificial-intelligence community has labored, with mixed success, on nudging computers to ascertain directly the identity of objects within an image, whether they are cats or national flags. This approach correlates the shapes in a picture with geometric models of real-world objects. The program can then deduce that a pink or brown cylinder, say, is a human arm.

One example is software that looks for naked people, a program that is the work of David A. Forsyth of Berkeley and Margaret M. Fleck of the University of Iowa. The software begins by analyzing the color and texture of a photograph. When it finds matches for flesh colors, it runs an algorithm that looks for cylindrical areas that might correspond to an arm or leg. It then seeks other flesh-colored cylinders, positioned at certain angles, which might confirm the presence of limbs. In a test last fall, the program picked out 43 percent of the 565 naked people among a group of 4,854 images, a high percentage for this type of complex image analysis. It registered, moreover, only a 4 percent false positive rate among the 4,289 images that did not contain naked bodies. The nudes were downloaded from the Web; the other photographs came primarily from commercial databases.

The challenges of computer vision will most likely remain for a decade or so to come. Searches capable of distinguishing clearly among nudes, marmalades and national flags are still an unrealized dream. As time goes on, though, researchers would like to give the programs that collect information from the Internet the ability to understand what they see.

Further Reading

The Harvest Information Discovery and Access System. C. M. Bowman et al. in *Computer Networks and ISDN Systems*, Vol. 28, Nos. 1–2, pages 119–125; December 1995.

The Harvest Information Discovery and Access System is available on the World Wide Web at **http:// harvest.transarc.com**

The Warwick Metadata Workshop: A Framework for the Deployment of Resource Description. Lorcan Dempsey and Stuart L. Weibel in *D-lib Magazine*, July–August 1996. Available on the World Wide Web at **http://www.dlib.org/dlib/ july96/07contents.html**

The Warwick Framework: A Container Architecture for Diverse Sets of Metadata. Carl Lagoze, ibid.

"XML and the Second-Generation Web"

4.

by Jon Bosak and Tim Bray

The combination of hypertext and a global Internet started a revolution.
A new ingredient, XML, is poised to finish the job

Give people a few hints, and they can figure out the rest. They can look at this page, see some large type followed by blocks of small type and know that they are looking at the start of a magazine article. They can look at a list of groceries and see shopping instructions. They can look at some rows of numbers and understand the state of their bank account.

Computers, of course, are not that smart; they need to be told exactly what things are, how they are related and how to deal with them. Extensible Markup Language (XML for short) is a new language designed to do just that, to make information self-describing. This simple-sounding change in how computers communicate has the potential to extend the Internet beyond information delivery to many other kinds of human activity. Indeed, since XML was completed in early 1998 by the World Wide Web Consortium (usually called the W3C), the standard has spread like wildfire through science and into industries ranging from manufacturing to medicine.

The enthusiastic response is fueled by a hope that XML will solve some of the Web's biggest problems.

These are widely known: the Internet is a speed-of-light
network that often moves at a crawl; and although
nearly every kind of information is available on-line,
it can be maddeningly difficult to find the one piece
you need.

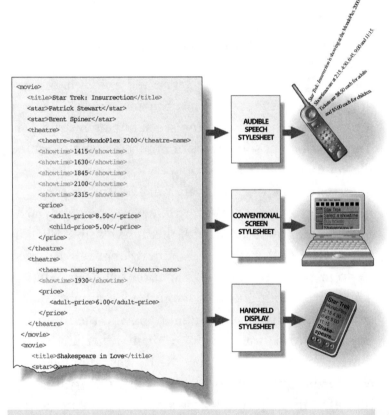

MARKED UP WITH XML TAGS, one file—containing, say, movie listings for
an entire city—can be displayed on a wide variety of devices. "Stylesheets"
can filter, reorder and render the listings as a Web page with graphics for a
desktop computer, as a text-only list for a handheld organizer and even as
audible speech for a telephone.

Both problems arise in large part from the nature of the Web's main language, HTML (shorthand for Hypertext Markup Language). Although HTML is the most successful electronic-publishing language ever invented, it is superficial: in essence, it describes how a Web browser should arrange text, images and push-buttons on a page. HTML's concern with appearances makes it relatively easy to learn, but it also has its costs.

One is the difficulty in creating a Web site that functions as more than just a fancy fax machine that sends documents to anyone who asks. People and companies want Web sites that take orders from customers, transmit medical records, even run factories and scientific instruments from half a world away. HTML was never designed for such tasks.

So although your doctor may be able to pull up your drug reaction history on his Web browser, he cannot then e-mail it to a specialist and expect her to be able to paste the records directly into her hospital's database. Her computer would not know what to make of the information, which to its eyes would be no more intelligible than <H1>blah blah </H1> <BOLD>blah blah blah </BOLD>. As programming legend Brian Kernighan once noted, the problem with "What You See Is What You Get" is that what you see is all you've got.

Those angle-bracketed labels in the example just above are called tags. HTML has no tag for a drug reaction, which highlights another of its limitations: it is inflexible. Adding a new tag involves a bureaucratic process that can take so long that few attempt it.

And yet every application, not just the interchange of medical records, needs its own tags.

Thus the slow pace of today's on-line bookstores, mail-order catalogues and other interactive Web sites. Change the quantity or shipping method of your order, and to see the handful of digits that have changed in the total, you must ask a distant, overburdened server to send you an entirely new page, graphics and all. Meanwhile your own high-powered machine sits waiting idly, because it has only been told about <H1>s and <BOLD>s, not about prices and shipping options.

Thus also the dissatisfying quality of Web searches. Because there is no way to mark something as a price, it is effectively impossible to use price information in your searches.

Something Old, Something New

The solution, in theory, is very simple: use tags that say what the information is, not what it looks like. For example, label the parts of an order for a shirt not as boldface, paragraph, row and column—what HTML offers—but as price, size, quantity and color. A program can then recognize this document as a customer order and do whatever it needs to do: display it one way or display it a different way or put it through a book-keeping system or make a new shirt show up on your doorstep tomorrow.

We, as members of a dozen-strong W3C working group, began crafting such a solution in 1996. Our idea was powerful but not entirely original. For generations, printers scribbled notes on manuscripts to instruct the typesetters. This "markup" evolved on its own until 1986, when, after decades of work, the International Organization for Standardization (ISO) approved a system for the creation of new markup languages.

Named Standard Generalized Markup Language, or SGML, this language for describing languages—a metalanguage—has since proved useful in many large publishing applications. Indeed, HTML was defined using SGML. The only problem with SGML is that it is *too* general—full of clever features designed to minimize keystrokes in an era when every byte had to be accounted for. It is more complex than Web browsers can cope with.

Our team created XML by removing frills from SGML to arrive at a more streamlined, digestible metalanguage. XML consists of rules that anyone can follow to create a markup language from scratch. The rules ensure that a single compact program, often called a parser, can process all these new languages.

Consider again the doctor who wants to e-mail your medical record to a specialist. If the medical profession uses XML to hammer out a markup language for encoding medical records—and in fact several groups have already started work on this— then your doctor's e-mail could contain <patient> <name> blah blah </name> <drug-allergy> blah blah blah </drug-allergy> </patient>. Programming any computer to recognize this standard medical notation and to add this vital statistic to its database becomes straightforward.

Just as HTML created a way for every computer user to read Internet documents, XML makes it possible, despite the Babel of incompatible computer systems, to create an Esperanto that all can read and write. Unlike most computer data formats, XML markup also makes sense to humans, because it consists of nothing more than ordinary text.

The unifying power of XML arises from a few well-chosen rules. One is that tags almost always come in pairs. Like parentheses, they surround the text to which they apply. And like quotation marks, tag pairs can be nested inside one another to multiple levels.

The nesting rule automatically forces a certain simplicity on every XML document, which takes on the structure known in computer science as a tree. As with a genealogical tree, each graphic and bit of text in the document represents a parent, child or sibling of some other element; relationships are unambiguous. Trees cannot represent every kind of information, but they can represent most kinds that we need computers to understand. Trees, moreover, are extraordinarily convenient for programmers. If your bank statement is in the form of a tree, it is a simple matter to write a bit of software that will reorder the transactions or display just the cleared checks.

Another source of XML's unifying strength is its reliance on a new standard called Unicode, a character-encoding system that supports intermingling of text in all the world's major languages. In HTML, as in most word processors, a document is generally in one particular language, whether that be English or Japanese or Arabic. If your software cannot read the characters of that language, then you cannot use the document. The situation can be even worse: software made for use in Taiwan often cannot read mainland-Chinese texts because of incompatible encodings. But software that reads XML properly can deal with any combination of any of these character sets. Thus, XML enables exchange of information not only between different computer systems but also across national and cultural boundaries.

An End to the World Wide Wait

As XML spreads, the Web should be come noticeably more responsive. At present, computing devices connected to the Web, whether they are powerful desktop computers or tiny pocket planners, cannot do much more than get a form, fill it out and then swap it back and forth with a Web server until a job is completed. But the structural and semantic information that can be added with XML allows these devices to do a great deal of processing on the spot. That not only will take a big load off Web servers but also should reduce network traffic dramatically.

To understand why, imagine going to an on-line travel agency and asking for all the flights from London to New York on July 4. You would probably receive a list several times longer than your screen could display. You could shorten the list by fine-tuning the departure time, price or airline, but to do that, you would have to send a request across the Internet to the travel agency and wait for its answer. If, however, the long list of flights had been sent in XML, then the travel agency could have sent a small Java program along with the flight records that you could use to sort and winnow them in microseconds, without ever involving the server. Multiply this by a few million Web users, and the global efficiency gains become dramatic.

As more of the information on the Net is labeled with industry-specific XML tags, it will become easier to find exactly what you need. Today an Internet search for "stockbroker jobs" will inundate you with advertisements but probably turn up few job listings—most will be hidden inside the classified ad services of newspaper Web sites, out of a search robot's reach. But the Newspaper Association of America is even now building an XML-based markup language for classified ads that promises to make such searches much more effective.

Even that is just an intermediate step. Librarians figured out a long time ago that the way to find information in a hurry is to look not at the information itself but rather at much smaller, more focused sets of data that guide you to the useful sources: hence the library card catalogue. Such information about information is called metadata.

From the outset, part of the XML project has been to create a sister standard for metadata. The Resource

Description Framework (RDF), finished this past February, should do for Web data what catalogue cards do for library books. Deployed across the Web, RDF metadata will make retrieval far faster and more accurate than it is now. Because the Web has no librarians and every Webmaster wants, above all else, to be found, we expect that RDF will achieve a typically astonishing Internet growth rate once its power becomes apparent.

There are of course other ways to find things besides searching. The Web is after all a "hypertext," its billions of pages connected by hyperlinks—those underlined words you click on to get whisked from one to the next. Hyperlinks, too, will do more when powered by XML. A standard for XML-based hypertext, named XLink and due later this year from the W3C, will allow you to choose from a list of multiple destinations. Other kinds of hyperlinks will insert text or images right where you click, instead of forcing you to leave the page.

Perhaps most useful, XLink will enable authors to use indirect links that point to entries in some central database rather than to the linked pages themselves. When a page's address changes, the author will be able to update all the links that point to it by editing just one database record. This should help eliminate the familiar "404 File Not Found" error that signals a broken hyperlink.

The combination of more efficient processing, more accurate searching and more flexible linking will revolutionize the structure of the Web and make possible completely new ways of accessing information. Users will find this new Web faster, more powerful and more useful than the Web of today.

Some Assembly Required

Of course, it is not quite that simple. XML does allow anyone to design a new, custom-built language, but designing good languages is a challenge that should not be undertaken lightly. And the design is just the beginning: the meanings of your tags are not going to be obvious to other people unless you write some prose to explain them, nor to computers unless you write some software to process them.

A moment's thought reveals why. If all it took to teach a computer to handle a purchase order were to label it with <purchase-order> tags, we wouldn't need XML. We wouldn't even need programmers—the machines would be smart enough to take care of themselves.

What XML does is less magical but quite effective nonetheless. It lays down ground rules that clear away a layer of programming details so that people with similar interests can concentrate on the hard part—agreeing on how they want to represent the information they commonly exchange. This is not an easy problem to solve, but it is not a new one, either.

Such agreements will be made, because the proliferation of incompatible computer systems has imposed delays, costs and confusion on nearly every area of human activity. People want to share ideas and do business without all having to use the same computers; activity-specific interchange languages go a long way toward making that possible. Indeed, a shower of new acronyms ending in "ML" testifies to the inventiveness

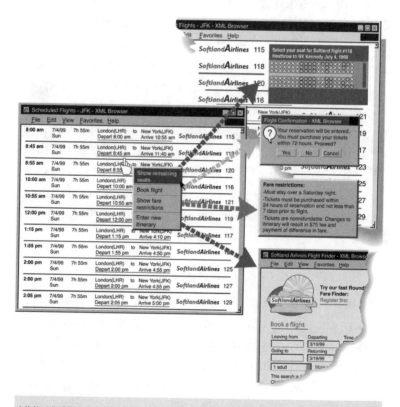

XML HYPERLINK can open a menu of several options. One option might insert an image, such as a plane seating chart, into the current page. Others could run a small program to book a flight or reveal hidden text. The links can also connect to other pages.

unleashed by XML in the sciences, in business and in the scholarly disciplines.

Before they can draft a new XML language, designers must agree on three things: which tags will be allowed, how tagged elements may nest within one another and how they should be processed. The first two—the language's vocabulary and structure—are typically codified in a Document Type Definition, or DTD. The XML standard does not compel language designers to use DTDs, but most new languages will probably have them, because they make it much easier for programmers to write software that understands the markup and does intelligent things with it.

Programmers will also need a set of guidelines that describe, in human language, what all the tags mean. HTML, for instance, has a DTD but also hundreds of pages of descriptive prose that programmers refer to when they write browsers and other Web software.

A Question of Style

For users, it is what those programs do, not what the descriptions say, that is important. In many cases, people will want software to display XML-encoded information to human readers. But XML tags offer no inherent clues about how the information should look on screen or on paper.

This is actually an advantage for publishers, who would often like to "write once and publish everywhere"—to distill the substance of a publication and then pour it into myriad forms, both printed and electronic. XML lets them do this by tagging content to describe its meaning, independent of the display medium. Publishers can then apply rules organized into "stylesheets" to reformat the work automatically for various devices. The standard now being developed for XML stylesheets is called the Extensible Stylesheet Language, or XSL.

The latest versions of several Web browsers can read an XML document, fetch the appropriate stylesheet, and use it to sort and format the information on the screen. The reader might never know that he is looking at XML rather than HTML—except that XML-based sites run faster and are easier to use.

People with visual disabilities gain a free benefit from this approach to publishing. Stylesheets will let them render XML into Braille or audible speech. The advantages extend to others as well: commuters who want to surf the Web in their cars may also find it handy to have pages read aloud.

Although the Web has been a boon to science and to scholarship, it is commerce (or rather the expectation of future commercial gain) that has fueled its lightning growth. The recent surge in retail sales over the Web has drawn much attention, but business-to-business commerce is moving on-line at least as quickly. The flow of goods through the manufacturing process, for example, begs for automation. But schemes that rely on complex, direct program-to-program interaction have not worked well in practice, because they depend on a uniformity of processing that does not exist.

For centuries, humans have successfully done business by exchanging standardized documents: purchase orders, invoices, manifests, receipts and so on. Documents work for commerce because they do not require the parties involved to know about one another's internal procedures. Each record exposes

New Languages for Science

XML offers a particularly convenient way for scientists to exchange theories, calculations and experimental results. Mathematicians, among others, have long been frustrated by Web browsers' ablity to display mathematical expressions only as pictures. **MathML** now allows them to insert equations into their Web pages with a few lines of simple text. Readers can then paste those expressions directly into algebra software for calculation or graphing.

Chemists have gone a step further, developing new browser programs for their XML-based **Chemical Markup Language** (CML) that graphically render the molecular structure of compounds described in CML Web pages. Both CML and **Astronomy Markup Language** will help researchers sift quickly through reams of journal citations to find just the papers that apply to the object of their study. Astronomers, for example, can enter the sky coordinates of a galaxy to pull up a list of images, research papers and instrument data about that heavenly body.

XML will be helpful for running experiments as well as analyzing their results. National Aeronautics and Space Administration engineers began work last year on **Astronomical Instrument ML** (AIML) as a way to enable scientists on the ground to control the SOFIA infrared telescope as it flies on a Boeing 747. AIML should eventually allow astronomers all over the world to control telescopes and perhaps even satellites through straightforward Internet browser software.

Geneticists may soon be using **Biosequence ML** (BSML) to exchange and manipulate the flood of information produced by gene-mapping and gene-sequencing projects. A BSML browser built and distributed free by Visual Genomics in Columbus, Ohio, lets researchers search through vast databases of genetic code and display the resulting snippets as meaningful maps and charts rather than as obtuse strings of letters.

—*The Editors*

exactly what its recipient needs to know and no more. The exchange of documents is probably the right way to do business on-line, too. But this was not the job for which HTML was built.

XML, in contrast, was designed for document exchange, and it is becoming clear that universal electronic commerce will rely heavily on a flow of agreements, expressed in millions of XML documents pulsing around the Internet.

Thus, for its users, the XML-powered Web will be faster, friendlier and a better place to do business. Web site designers, on the other hand, will find it more demanding. Battalions of programmers will be needed to exploit new XML languages to their fullest. And although the day of the self-trained Web hacker is not yet over, the species is endangered. Tomorrow's Web designers will need to be versed not just in the production of words and graphics but also in the construction of multilayered, interdependent systems of DTDs, data trees, hyperlink structures, metadata and stylesheets— a more robust infrastructure for the Web's second generation.

The Authors

JON BOSAK and *TIM BRAY* played crucial roles in the development of XML. Bosak, an on-line information technology architect at Sun Microsystems in Mountain View, Calif., organized and led the World Wide Web Consortium working group that created XML. He is

currently chair of the W3C XML Coordination Group
and a representative to the Organization for the
Advancement of Structured Information Standards.
Bray is co-editor of the *XML 1.0* specification and the
related *Namespaces in XML* and serves as co-chair of
the W3C XML Syntax Working Group. He managed the
New Oxford English Dictionary Project at the University
of Waterloo in 1986, co-founded Open Text Corporation
in 1989 and launched Textuality, a programming firm
in Vancouver, B.C., in 1996.

"Hypersearching
5. the Web"

by Members of the "Clever" Project

With the volume of on-line information in cyberspace growing at a breakneck pace, more effective search tools are desperately needed. A new technique analyzes how Web pages are linked together

Every day the World Wide Web grows by roughly a million electronic pages, adding to the hundreds of millions already on-line. This staggering volume of information is loosely held together by more than a billion annotated connections, called hyperlinks. For the first time in history, millions of people have virtually instant access from their homes and offices to the creative output of a significant—and growing—fraction of the planet's population.

But because of the Web's rapid, chaotic growth, the resulting network of information lacks organization and structure. In fact, the Web has evolved into a global mess of previously unimagined proportions. Web pages can be written in any language, dialect or style by individuals with any background, education, culture, interest and motivation. Each page might range from a few characters to a few hundred thousand, containing truth, falsehood, wisdom, propaganda or sheer nonsense. How, then, can one extract from this digital morass high-quality, relevant pages in response to a specific need for certain information?

In the past, people have relied on search engines that hunt for specific words or terms. But such text

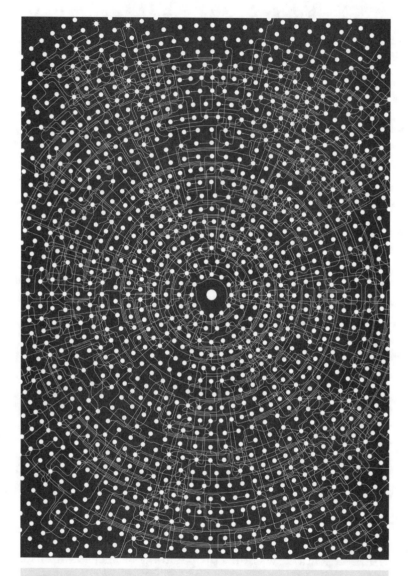

WEB PAGES (*dots*) are scattered over the Internet with little structure, making it difficult for a person in the center of this electronic clutter to find only the information desired. Although this diagram shows just hundreds of pages, the World Wide Web currently contains more than 300 million of them. Nevertheless, an analysis of the way in which certain pages are linked to one another can reveal a hidden order.

searches frequently retrieve tens of thousands of pages, many of them useless. How can people quickly locate only the information they need and trust that it is authentic and reliable?

We have developed a new kind of search engine that exploits one of the Web's most valuable resources—its myriad hyperlinks. By analyzing these interconnections, our system automatically locates two types of pages: authorities and hubs. The former are deemed to be the best sources of information on a particular topic; the latter are collections of links to those locations. Our methodology should enable users to locate much of the information they desire quickly and efficiently.

The Challenges of Search Engines

Computer disks have become increasingly inexpensive, enabling the storage of a large portion of the Web at a single site. At its most basic level, a search engine maintains a list, for every word, of all known Web pages containing that word. Such a collection of lists is known as an index. So if people are interested in learning about acupuncture, they can access the "acupuncture" list to find all Web pages containing that word.

Creating and maintaining this index is highly challenging [see "Searching the Internet," by Clifford Lynch; SCIENTIFIC AMERICAN, March 1997], and determining what information to return in response to user requests remains daunting. Consider the unambiguous query for information on "Nepal Airways," the airline

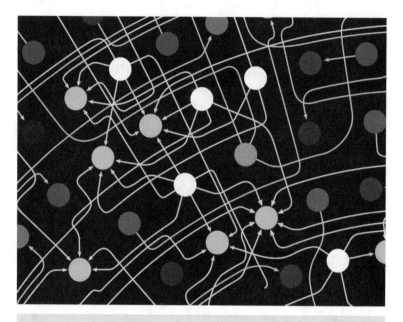

FINDING authorities and hubs can be tricky because of the circular way in which they are defined: an authority is a page that is pointed to by many hubs; a hub is a site that links to many authorities. The process, however, can be performed mathematically. Clever, a prototype search engine, assigns initial scores to candidate Web pages on a particular topic. Clever then revises those numbers in repeated series of calculations, with each iteration dependent on the values of the previous round. The computations continue until the scores eventually settle on their final values, which can then be used to determine the best authorities and hubs.

company. Of the roughly 100 (at the time of this writing) Web pages containing the phrase, how does a search engine decide which 20 or so are the best? One difficulty is that there is no exact and mathematically precise measure of "best"; indeed, it lies in the eye of the beholder.

Search engines such as AltaVista, Infoseek, HotBot, Lycos and Excite use heuristics to determine the way in which to order—and thereby prioritize—pages. These rules of thumb are collectively known as a ranking function, which must apply not only to relatively specific and straightforward queries ("Nepal Airways") but also to much more general requests, such as for "aircraft," a word that appears in more than a million Web pages. How should a search engine choose just 20 from such a staggering number?

Simple heuristics might rank pages by the number of times they contain the query term, or they may favor instances in which that text appears earlier. But such approaches can sometimes fail spectacularly. Tom Wolfe's book *The Kandy-Kolored Tangerine-Flake Streamline Baby* would, if ranked by such heuristics, be deemed very relevant to the query "hernia," because it begins by repeating that word dozens of times. Numerous extensions to these rules of thumb abound, including approaches that give more weight to words that appear in titles, in section headings or in a larger font.

Such strategies are routinely thwarted by many commercial Web sites that design their pages in certain ways specifically to elicit favorable rankings. Thus, one encounters pages whose titles are "cheap airfares cheap airfares cheap airfares." Some sites write other carefully chosen phrases many times over in colors and fonts that are invisible to human viewers. This practice, called spamming, has become one of the main reasons why it is currently so difficult to maintain an effective search engine.

Spamming aside, even the basic assumptions of conventional text searches are suspect. To wit, pages that are highly relevant will not always contain the query term, and others that do may be worthless. A major cause of this problem is that human language, in all its richness, is awash in synonymy (different words having the same meaning) and polysemy (the same word having multiple meanings). Because of the former, a query for "automobile" will miss a deluge of pages that lack that word but instead contain "car." The latter manifests itself in a simple query for "jaguar," which will retrieve thousands of pages about the automobile, the jungle cat and the National Football League team, among other topics.

One corrective strategy is to augment search techniques with stored information about semantic relations between words. Such compilations, typically constructed by a team of linguists, are sometimes known as semantic networks, following the seminal work on the WordNet project by George A. Miller and his colleagues at Princeton University. An index-based engine with access to a semantic network could, on receiving the query for "automobile," first determine that "car" is equivalent and then retrieve all Web pages containing either word. But this process is a double-edged sword: it helps with synonymy but can aggravate polysemy.

Even as a cure for synonymy, the solution is problematic. Constructing and maintaining a semantic network that is exhaustive and cross-cultural (after all, the Web knows no geographical boundaries) are formidable tasks. The process is especially difficult on the Internet, where a whole new language is evolving—words such as "FAQs," "zines" and "bots" have emerged, whereas other words such as "surf" and "browse" have taken on additional meanings.

Our work on the Clever project at IBM originated amid this perplexing array of issues. Early on, we realized that the current scheme of indexing and retrieving a page based solely on the text it contained ignores more than a billion carefully placed hyperlinks that reveal the relations between pages. But how exactly should this information be used?

When people perform a search for "Harvard," many of them want to learn more about the Ivy League school. But more than a million locations contain "Harvard," and the university's home page is not the one that uses it the most frequently, the earliest or in any other way deemed especially significant by traditional ranking functions. No entirely internal feature of that home page truly seems to reveal its importance.

Indeed, people design Web pages with all kinds of objectives in mind. For instance, large corporations want their sites to convey a certain feel and project a specific image—goals that might be very different from that of describing what the company does. Thus, IBM's home page does not contain the word "computer." For these types of situations, conventional search techniques are doomed from the start.

To address such concerns, human architects of search engines have been tempted to intervene. After all, they believe they know what the appropriate responses to certain queries should be, and developing a ranking function that will automatically produce those results has been a troublesome undertaking. So they could maintain a list of queries like "Harvard" for which they will override the judgment of the search engine with predetermined "right" answers.

This approach is being taken by a number of search engines. In fact, a service such as Yahoo! contains only human-selected pages. But there are countless possible queries. How, with a limited number of human experts, can one maintain all these lists of precomputed responses, keeping them reasonably complete and up-to-date, as the Web meanwhile grows by a million pages a day?

Searching with Hyperlinks

In our work, we have been attacking the problem in a different way. We have developed an automatic technique for finding the most central, authoritative sites on broad search topics by making use of hyperlinks, one of the Web's most precious resources. It is the hyperlinks, after all, that pull together the hundreds of millions of pages into a web of knowledge. It is through these connections that users browse, serendipitously discovering valuable information through the pointers and recommendations of people they have never met.

The underlying assumption of our approach views each link as an implicit endorsement of the location to which it points. Consider the Web site of a human-rights activist that directs people to the home page of Amnesty International. In this case, the reference clearly signifies approval.

Of course, a link may also exist purely for navigational purposes ("Click here to return to the main menu"), as a paid advertisement ("The vacation of your dreams is only a click away") or as a stamp of disapproval ("Surf to this site to see what this fool says"). We believe, however, that in aggregate—that is, when a large enough number is considered—Web links do confer authority.

In addition to expert sites that have garnered many recommendations, the Web is full of another type of page: hubs that link to those prestigious locations, tacitly radiating influence outward to them. Hubs appear in guises ranging from professionally assembled lists on commercial sites to inventories of "My Favorite Links" on personal home pages. So even if we find it difficult to define "authorities" and "hubs" in isolation, we can state this much: a respected authority is a page that is referred to by many good hubs; a useful hub is a location that points to many valuable authorities.

These definitions look hopelessly circular. How could they possibly lead to a computational method of identifying both authorities and hubs? Thinking of the problem intuitively, we devised the following algorithm. To start off, we look at a set of candidate pages about a particular topic, and for each one we make our best guess about how good a hub it is and how good an authority it is. We then use these initial estimates to jump-start a two-step iterative process.

First, we use the current guesses about the authorities to improve the estimates of hubs—we locate all the best authorities, see which pages point to them and call those locations good hubs. Second, we take the updated hub information to refine our guesses about the authorities—we determine where the best hubs point most heavily and call these the good authorities. Repeating these steps several times fine-tunes the results.

We have implemented this algorithm in Clever, a prototype search engine. For any query of a topic—say, acupuncture—Clever first obtains a list of 200 pages from a standard text index such as AltaVista. The system then augments these by adding all pages that link to and from that 200. In our experience, the resulting collection, called the root set, will typically contain between 1,000 and 5,000 pages.

For each of these, Clever assigns initial numerical hub and authority scores. The system then refines the values: the authority score of each page is updated to be the sum of the hub scores of other locations that point to it; a hub score is revised to be the sum of the authority scores of locations to which a page points. In other words, a page that has many high-scoring hubs pointing to it earns a higher authority score; a location that points to many high-scoring authorities garners a higher hub score. Clever repeats these calculations until the scores have more or less settled on their final values, from which the best authorities and hubs can be determined. (Note that the computations do not preclude a particular page from achieving a top rank in both categories, as sometimes occurs.)

The algorithm might best be understood in visual terms. Picture the Web as a vast network of innumerable sites, all interconnected in a seemingly random fashion. For a given set of pages containing a certain word or term, Clever zeroes in on the densest pattern of links between those pages.

As it turns out, the iterative summation of hub and authority scores can be analyzed with stringent mathematics. Using linear algebra, we can represent the process as the repeated multiplication of a vector (specifically, a row of numbers representing the hub or authority scores) by a matrix (a two-dimensional array of numbers representing the hyperlink structure of the root set). The final results of the process are hub and authority vectors that have equilibrated to certain numbers—values that reveal which pages are the best hubs and authorities, respectively. (In the world of linear algebra, such a stabilized row of numbers is called an eigenvector; it can be thought of as the solution to a system of equations defined by the matrix.)

With further linear algebraic analysis, we have shown that the iterative process will rapidly settle to a relatively steady set of hub and authority scores. For our purposes, a root set of 3,000 pages requires about five rounds of calculations. Furthermore, the results are generally independent of the initial estimates of scores used to start the process. The method will work even if the values are all initially set to be equal to 1. So the final hub and authority scores are intrinsic to the collection of pages in the root set.

A useful by-product of Clever's iterative processing is that the algorithm naturally separates Web sites into clusters. A search for information on abortion, for example, results in two types of locations, pro-life and pro-choice, because pages from one group are more likely to link to one another than to those from the other community.

From a larger perspective, Clever's algorithm reveals the underlying structure of the World Wide Web. Although the Internet has grown in a hectic, willy-nilly fashion, it does indeed have an inherent—albeit inchoate—order based on how pages are linked.

The Link to Citation Analysis

Methodologically, the Clever algorithm has close ties to citation analysis, the study of patterns of how scientific papers make reference to one another. Perhaps the field's best-known measure of a journal's importance is the "impact factor." Developed by Eugene Garfield, a noted information scientist and founder of *Science Citation Index,* the metric essentially judges a publication by the number of citations it receives.

On the Web, the impact factor would correspond to the ranking of a page simply by a tally of the number of links that point to it. But this approach is typically not appropriate, because it can favor universally popular locations, such as the home page of the *New York Times,* regardless of the specific query topic.

Even in the area of citation analysis, researchers have attempted to improve Garfield's measure, which counts each reference equally. Would not a better strategy give additional weight to citations from a journal deemed more important? Of course, the difficulty with this approach is that it leads to a circular definition of "importance," similar to the problem we encountered in specifying hubs and authorities. As early as 1976 Gabriel Pinski and Francis Narin of CHI Research in Haddon Heights, N.J., overcame this hurdle by developing an iterated method for computing a stable set of adjusted scores, which they termed influence weights. In contrast to our work, Pinski and Narin did not invoke a distinction between authorities and hubs. Their method essentially passes weight directly from one good authority to another.

This difference raises a fundamental point about the Web versus traditional printed scientific literature. In cyberspace, competing authorities (for example, Netscape and Microsoft on the topic of browsers) frequently do not acknowledge one another's existence, so they can be connected only by an intermediate layer of hubs. Rival prominent scientific journals, on the other hand, typically do a fair amount of cross-citation, making the role of hubs much less crucial.

A number of groups are also investigating the power of hyperlinks for searching the Web. Sergey

Brin and Lawrence Page of Stanford University, for instance, have developed a search engine dubbed Google that implements a link-based ranking measure related to the influence weights of Pinski and Narin. The Stanford scientists base their approach on a model of a Web surfer who follows links and makes occasional haphazard jumps, arriving at certain places more frequently than others. Thus, Google finds a single type of universally important page—intuitively, locations that are heavily visited in a random traversal of the Web's link structure. In practice, for each Web page Google basically sums the scores of other locations pointing to it. So, when presented with a specific query, Google can respond by quickly retrieving all pages containing the search text and listing them according to their preordained ranks.

Google and Clever have two main differences. First, the former assigns initial rankings and retains them independently of any queries, whereas the latter assembles a different root set for each search term and then prioritizes those pages in the context of that particular query. Consequently, Google's approach enables faster response. Second, Google's basic philosophy is to look only in the forward direction, from link to link. In contrast, Clever also looks backward from an authoritative page to see what locations are pointing there. In this sense, Clever takes advantage of the sociological phenomenon that humans are innately motivated to create hublike content expressing their expertise on specific topics.

The Search Continues

We are exploring a number of ways to enhance Clever. A fundamental direction in our overall approach is the integration of text and hyperlinks. One strategy is to view certain links as carrying more weight than others, based on the relevance of the text in the referring Web location. Specifically, we can analyze the contents of the pages in the root set for the occurrences and relative positions of the query topic and use this information to assign numerical weights to some of the connections between those pages. If the query text appeared frequently and close to a link, for instance, the corresponding weight would be increased.

Our preliminary experiments suggest that this refinement substantially increases the focus of the search results. (A shortcoming of Clever has been that for a narrow topic, such as Frank Lloyd Wright's house Fallingwater, the system sometimes broadens its search and retrieves information on a general subject, such as American architecture.) We are investigating other improvements, and given the many styles of authorship on the Web, the weighting of links might incorporate page content in a variety of ways.

We have also begun to construct lists of Web resources, similar to the guides put together manually by employees of companies such as Yahoo! and Infoseek. Our early results indicate that automatically compiled lists can be competitive with handcrafted ones. Furthermore, through this work we have found that the Web teems with tightly knit groups of people, many with offbeat common interests (such as weekend sumo enthusiasts who don bulky plastic outfits and wrestle each other for fun), and we are currently investigating efficient and automatic methods for uncovering these hidden communities.

The World Wide Web of today is dramatically different from that of just five years ago. Predicting what it will be like in another five years seems futile. Will even the basic act of indexing the Web soon become infeasible? And if so, will our notion of searching the Web undergo fundamental changes? For now, the one thing we feel certain in saying is that the Web's relentless growth will continue to generate computational challenges for wading through the ever increasing volume of on-line information.

The Authors

The *Clever* Project: Soumen Chakrabarti, Byron Dom, S. Ravi Kumar, Prabhakar Raghavan, Sridhar Rajagopalan and Andrew Tomkins are research staff members at the IBM Almaden Research Center in San Jose, Calif. Jon M. Kleinberg is an assistant professor in the computer science department at Cornell University. David Gibson is completing his Ph.D. at the computer science division at the University of California, Berkeley.

The authors began their quest for exploiting the hyperlink structure of the World Wide Web three years ago, when they first sought to develop improved techniques for finding information in the clutter of cyberspace. Their work originated with the following question: If computation were not a bottleneck, what would be the most effective search algorithm? In other words, could they build a better search engine if the processing didn't have to be instantaneous? The result was the algorithm described in this article. Recently the research team has been investigating the Web phenomenon of cybercommunities.

Further Reading

Search Engine Watch (www.searchenginewatch.com) contains information on the latest progress in search engines. The WordNet project is described in *WordNet: An Electronic Lexical Database* (MIT Press, 1998), edited by Christiane Fellbaum. The iterative method for determining hubs and authorities first appeared in Jon M. Kleinberg's paper "Authoritative Sources in a Hyperlinked Environment" in *Proceedings of the 9th ACM-SIAM Symposium on Discrete Algorithms,* edited by Howard Karloff (SIAM/ACM–SIGACT, 1998). Improvements to the algorithm are described at the Web site of the IBM Almaden Research Center (www. almaden.ibm.com/cs/k53/clever.html). *Introduction to Informetrics* (Elsevier Science Publishers, 1990), by Leo Egghe and Ronald Rousseau, provides a good overview of citation analysis. Information on the Google project at Stanford University can be obtained from www.google.com on the World Wide Web.

6. "The Semantic Web"

by Tim Berners-Lee, James Hendler and Ora Lassila

*A new form of Web content that is meaningful
to computers will unleash a revolution of new possibilities*

THE ENTERTAINMENT SYSTEM was belting out the
Beatles' "We Can Work It Out" when the phone rang.
When Pete answered, his phone turned the sound
down by sending a message to all the other *local*
devices that had a *volume control*. His sister, Lucy,
was on the line from the doctor's office: "Mom needs
to see a specialist and then has to have a series of
physical therapy sessions. Biweekly or something.
I'm going to have my agent set up the appointments."
Pete immediately agreed to share the chauffeuring.

At the doctor's office, Lucy instructed her Semantic
Web agent through her handheld Web browser. The
agent promptly retrieved information about Mom's
prescribed treatment from the doctor's agent, looked
up several lists of *providers*, and checked for the ones
in-plan for Mom's insurance within a *20-mile radius*
of her *home* and with a *rating* of *excellent* or *very
good* on trusted rating services. It then began trying to
find a match between available *appointment times*
(supplied by the agents of individual providers through
their Web sites) and Pete's and Lucy's busy schedules.
(The emphasized keywords indicate terms whose

semantics, or meaning, were defined for the agent through the Semantic Web.)

In a few minutes the agent presented them with a plan. Pete didn't like it—University Hospital was all the way across town from Mom's place, and he'd be driving back in the middle of rush hour. He set his own agent to redo the search with stricter preferences about location and time. Lucy's agent, having complete trust in Pete's agent in the context of the present task, automatically assisted by supplying access certificates and shortcuts to the data it had already sorted through.

Almost instantly the new plan was presented: a much closer clinic and earlier times—but there were two warning notes. First, Pete would have to reschedule a couple of his *less important* appointments. He checked what they were—not a problem. The other was something about the insurance company's list failing to include this provider under *physical therapists*: "Service type and insurance plan status securely verified by other means," the agent reassured him. "(Details?)"

Lucy registered her assent at about the same moment Pete was muttering, "Spare me the details," and it was all set. (Of course, Pete couldn't resist the details and later that night had his agent explain how it had found that provider even though it wasn't on the proper list.)

Expressing Meaning

PETE AND LUCY could use their agents to carry out all these tasks thanks not to the World Wide Web of today but rather the Semantic Web that it will evolve into tomorrow. Most of the Web's content today is designed for humans to read, not for computer programs to manipulate meaningfully. Computers can adeptly parse Web pages for layout and routine processing— here a header, there a link to another page—but in general, computers have no reliable way to process the semantics: this is the home page of the Hartman and Strauss Physio Clinic, this link goes to Dr. Hartman's curriculum vitae.

The Semantic Web will bring structure to the meaningful content of Web pages, creating an environment where software agents roaming from page to page can readily carry out sophisticated tasks for users. Such an agent coming to the clinic's Web page will know not just that the page has keywords such as "treatment, medicine, physical, therapy" (as might be encoded today) but also that Dr. Hartman *works* at this clinic on *Mondays*, *Wednesdays* and *Fridays* and that the script takes a *date range* in *yyyy-mm-dd format* and returns *appointment times*. And it will "know" all this without needing artificial intelligence on the scale of 2001's Hal or *Star Wars*'s C-3PO. Instead these semantics were encoded into the Web page when the clinic's office manager (who never took Comp Sci 101) massaged it into shape using off-the-shelf software for writing Semantic Web pages along with resources listed on the Physical Therapy Association's site.

The Semantic Web is not a separate Web but an extension of the current one, in which information is given well-defined meaning, better enabling computers and people to work in cooperation. The first steps in weaving the Semantic Web into the structure of the existing Web are already under way. In the near future, these developments will usher in significant new functionality as machines become much better able to process and "understand" the data that they merely display at present.

The essential property of the World Wide Web is its universality. The power of a hypertext link is that "anything can link to anything." Web technology, therefore, must not discriminate between the scribbled draft and the polished performance, between commercial and academic information, or among cultures, languages, media and so on. Information varies along many axes. One of these is the difference between information produced primarily for human consumption

Overview/Semantic Web

- To date, the World Wide Web has developed most rapidly as a medium of documents for people rather than of information that can be manipulated automatically. By augmenting Web pages with data targeted at computers and by adding documents solely for computers, we will transform the Web into the Semantic Web.

- Computers will find the meaning of semantic data by following hyperlinks to definitions of key terms and rules for reasoning about them logically. The resulting infrastructure will spur the development of automated Web services such as highly functional agents.

- Ordinary users will compose Semantic Web pages and add new definitions and rules using off-the-shelf software that will assist with semantic markup.

and that produced mainly for machines. At one end of the scale we have everything from the five-second TV commercial to poetry. At the other end we have databases, programs and sensor output. To date, the Web has developed most rapidly as a medium of documents for people rather than for data and information that can be processed automatically. The Semantic Web aims to make up for this.

Like the Internet, the Semantic Web will be as decentralized as possible. Such Web-like systems generate a lot of excitement at every level, from major corporation to individual user, and provide benefits that are hard or impossible to predict in advance. Decentralization requires compromises: the Web had to throw away the ideal of total consistency of all of its interconnections, ushering in the infamous message "Error 404: Not Found" but allowing unchecked exponential growth.

Knowledge Representation

FOR THE SEMANTIC WEB to function, computers must have access to structured collections of information and sets of inference rules that they can use to conduct automated reasoning. Artificial-intelligence researchers have studied such systems since long before the Web was developed. Knowledge representation, as this technology is often called, is currently in a state comparable to that of hypertext before the advent of the Web: it is clearly a good idea, and some very nice demonstrations exist, but it has not yet changed the world. It contains the seeds of important applications, but to realize its full potential it must be linked into a single global system.

Traditional knowledge-representation systems typically have been centralized, requiring everyone to share exactly the same definition of common concepts such as "parent" or "vehicle." But central control is stifling, and increasing the size and scope of such a system rapidly becomes unmanageable.

Moreover, these systems usually carefully limit the questions that can be asked so that the computer can answer reliably—or answer at all. The problem is reminiscent of Gödel's theorem from mathematics: any system that is complex enough to be useful also encompasses unanswerable questions, much like sophisticated versions of the basic paradox "This sentence is false." To avoid such problems, traditional knowledge-representation systems generally each had their own narrow and idiosyncratic set of rules for making inferences about their data. For example, a genealogy system, acting on a database of family trees, might include the rule "a wife of an uncle is an aunt." Even if the data could be transferred from one system to another, the rules, existing in a completely different form, usually could not.

Semantic Web researchers, in contrast, accept that paradoxes and unanswerable questions are a price that must be paid to achieve versatility. We make the language for the rules as expressive as needed to allow the Web to reason as widely as desired. This philosophy is similar to that of the conventional Web: early in the Web's development, detractors pointed out that it could never be a well-organized library; without a central database and tree structure, one would never be sure of finding everything. They were right. But the expressive power of the system made vast amounts of information available, and search engines (which would have seemed quite impractical a decade ago) now produce remarkably complete indices of a lot of the material out there.

The challenge of the Semantic Web, therefore, is to provide a language that expresses both data and rules for reasoning about the data and that allows rules from any existing knowledge-representation system to be exported onto the Web.

Adding logic to the Web—the means to use rules to make inferences, choose courses of action and answer questions—is the task before the Semantic Web community at the moment. A mixture of mathematical and engineering decisions complicate this task. The logic must be powerful enough to describe complex properties of objects but not so powerful that agents can be tricked by being asked to consider a paradox. Fortunately, a large majority of the information we want to express is along the lines of "a hex-head bolt is a type of machine bolt," which is readily written in existing languages with a little extra vocabulary.

Two important technologies for developing the Semantic Web are already in place: eXtensible Markup Language (XML) and the Resource Description

Framework (RDF). XML lets everyone create their own tags—hidden labels such as <zip code> or <alma mater> that annotate Web pages or sections of text on a page. Scripts, or programs, can make use of these tags in sophisticated ways, but the script writer has to know what the page writer uses each tag for. In short, XML allows users to add arbitrary structure to their documents but says nothing about what the structures mean.

Meaning is expressed by RDF, which encodes it in sets of triples, each triple being rather like the subject, verb and object of an elementary sentence. These triples can be written using XML tags. In RDF, a document makes assertions that particular things (people, Web pages or whatever) have properties (such as "is a sister of," "is the author of") with certain values (another person, another Web page). This structure turns out to be a natural way to describe the vast majority of the data processed by machines. Subject and object are each identified by a Universal Resource Identifier (URI), just as used in a link on a Web page. (URLs, Uniform Resource Locators, are the most common type of URI.) The verbs are also identified by URIs, which enables anyone to define a new concept, a new verb, just by defining a URI for it somewhere on the Web.

Human language thrives when using the same term to mean somewhat different things, but automation does not. Imagine that I hire a clown messenger service to deliver balloons to my customers on their birthdays.

Glossary

HTML: Hypertext Markup Language. The language used to encode formatting, links and other features on Web pages. Uses standardized "tags" such as <H1> and <BODY> whose meaning and interpretation is set universally by the World Wide Web Consortium.

XML: eXtensible Markup Language. A markup language like HTML that lets individuals define and use their own tags. XML has no built-in mechanism to convey the meaning of the user's new tags to other users.

RESOURCE: Web jargon for any entity. Includes Web pages, parts of a Web page, devices, people and more.

URL: Uniform Resource Locator. The familiar codes (such as http://www.sciam.com/index.html) that are used in hyperlinks.

URI: Universal Resource Identifier. URLs are the most familiar type of URI. A URI defines or specifies an entity, not necessarily by naming its location on the Web.

RDF: Resource Description Framework. A scheme for defining information on the Web. RDF provides the technology for expressing the meaning of terms and concepts in a form that computers can readily process. RDF can use XML for its syntax and URIs to specify entities, concepts, properties and relations.

ONTOLOGIES: Collections of statements written in a language such as RDF that define the relations between concepts and specify logical rules for reasoning about them. Computers will "understand" the meaning of semantic data on a Web page by following links to specified ontologies.

AGENT: A piece of software that runs without direct human control or constant supervision to accomplish goals provided by a user. Agents typically collect, filter and process information found on the Web, sometimes with the help of other agents.

SERVICE DISCOVERY: The process of locating an agent or automated Web-based service that will perform a required function. Semantics will enable agents to describe to one another precisely what function they carry out and what input data are needed.

Unfortunately, the service transfers the addresses from my database to its database, not knowing that the "addresses" in mine are where bills are sent and that many of them are post office boxes. My hired clowns end up entertaining a number of postal workers—not necessarily a bad thing but certainly not the intended effect. Using a different URI for each specific concept solves that problem. An address that is a mailing address can be distinguished from one that is a street address, and both can be distinguished from an address that is a speech.

The triples of RDF form webs of information about related things. Because RDF uses URIs to encode this information in a document, the URIs ensure that concepts are not just words in a document but are tied to a unique definition that everyone can find on the Web. For example, imagine that we have access to a variety of databases with information about people, including their addresses. If we want to find people living in a specific zip code, we need to know which fields in each database represent names and which represent zip codes. RDF can specify that "(field 5 in database A) (is a field of type) (zip code)," using URIs rather than phrases for each term.

Ontologies

OF COURSE, THIS IS NOT the end of the story, because two databases may use different identifiers for what is in fact the same concept, such as *zip code*. A program that wants to compare or combine information across the two databases has to know that these two terms are being used to mean the same thing. Ideally, the program must have a way to discover such common meanings for whatever databases it encounters.

A solution to this problem is provided by the third basic component of the Semantic Web, collections of information called ontologies. In philosophy, an ontology is a theory about the nature of existence, of what types of things exist; ontology as a discipline studies such theories. Artificial-intelligence and Web researchers have co-opted the term for their own jargon, and for them an ontology is a document or file that formally defines the relations among terms. The most typical kind of ontology for the Web has a taxonomy and a set of inference rules.

The taxonomy defines classes of objects and relations among them. For example, an *address* may be defined as a type of *location*, and *city codes* may be defined to apply only to *locations*, and so on. Classes, subclasses and relations among entities are a very powerful tool for Web use. We can express a large number of relations among entities by assigning properties to classes and allowing subclasses to inherit such properties. If *city codes* must be of type *city* and cities generally have Web sites, we can discuss the Web site associated with a *city code* even if no database links a city code directly to a Web site.

Inference rules in ontologies supply further power. An ontology may express the rule "If a city code is associated with a state code, and an address uses that city code, then that address has the associated state code." A program could then readily deduce, for instance, that a Cornell University address, being in Ithaca, must be in New York State, which is in the U.S., and therefore should be formatted to U.S. standards. The computer doesn't truly "understand" any of this information, but it can now manipulate the terms much more effectively in ways that are useful and meaningful to the human user.

With ontology pages on the Web, solutions to terminology (and other) problems begin to emerge. The meaning of terms or XML codes used on a Web page can be defined by pointers from the page to an ontology. Of course, the same problems as before now arise if I point to an ontology that defines *addresses* as containing a *zip code* and you point to one that uses *postal code*. This kind of confusion can be resolved if ontologies (or other Web services) provide equivalence relations: one or both of our ontologies may contain the information that my *zip code* is equivalent to your *postal code*.

Our scheme for sending in the clowns to entertain my customers is partially solved when the two databases point to different definitions of *address*. The program, using distinct URIs for different concepts of *address*, will not confuse them and in fact will need to discover that the concepts are related at all. The program could then use a service that takes a list of postal *addresses* (defined in the first ontology) and converts it into a list of physical *addresses* (the second ontology) by recognizing and removing post office boxes and other unsuitable addresses. The structure and semantics provided by ontologies make it easier for an entrepreneur to provide such a service and can make its use completely transparent.

Ontologies can enhance the functioning of the Web in many ways. They can be used in a simple fashion to improve the accuracy of Web searches—the search program can look for only those pages that refer to a precise concept instead of all the ones using ambiguous keywords. More advanced applications will use ontologies to relate the information on a page to the associated knowledge structures and inference rules. An example of a page marked up for such use is online at http://www.cs.umd.edu/~hendler. If you send your Web browser to that page, you will see the normal Web page entitled "Dr. James A. Hendler." As a human, you can readily find the link to a short biographical note and read there that Hendler received his Ph.D. from Brown University. A computer program trying to find such information, however, would have to be very complex to guess that this information might be in a biography and to understand the English language used there.

For computers, the page is linked to an ontology page that defines information about computer science departments. For instance, professors work at universities and they generally have doctorates. Further markup on the page (not displayed by the typical Web browser) uses the ontology's concepts to specify that Hendler received his Ph.D. from the entity described at the URI http://www.brown.edu/—the Web page for Brown. Computers can also find that Hendler is a member of a particular research project, has a particular e-mail address, and so on. All that information is readily processed by a computer and could be used to answer queries (such as where Dr. Hendler received his degree) that currently would require a human to sift through the content of various pages turned up by a search engine.

In addition, this markup makes it much easier to develop programs that can tackle complicated questions whose answers do not reside on a single Web page. Suppose you wish to find the Ms. Cook you met at a trade conference last year. You don't remember her first name, but you remember that she worked for one of your clients and that her son was a student at your alma mater. An intelligent search program can sift through all the pages of people whose name is "Cook" (sidestepping all the pages relating to cooks, cooking, the Cook Islands and so forth), find the ones that mention working for a company that's on your list of clients and follow links to Web pages of their children to track down if any are in school at the right place.

Agents

THE REAL POWER of the Semantic Web will be realized when people create many programs that collect Web content from diverse sources, process the information and exchange the results with other programs. The effectiveness of such software agents will increase exponentially as more machine-readable Web content and automated services (including other agents) become available. The Semantic Web promotes this synergy: even agents that were not expressly designed to work together can transfer data among themselves when the data come with semantics.

An important facet of agents' functioning will be the exchange of "proofs" written in the Semantic Web's unifying language (the language that expresses logical inferences made using rules and information such as those specified by ontologies). For example, suppose Ms. Cook's contact information has been located by an online service, and to your great surprise it places her in Johannesburg. Naturally, you want to check this, so your computer asks the service for a proof of its answer, which it promptly provides by translating its internal reasoning into the Semantic Web's unifying language. An inference engine in your computer readily verifies that this Ms. Cook indeed matches the one you were seeking, and it can show you the relevant Web pages if you still have doubts. Although they are still far from plumbing the depths of the Semantic Web's potential, some programs can already exchange proofs in this way, using the current preliminary versions of the unifying language.

Another vital feature will be digital signatures, which are encrypted blocks of data that computers and agents can use to verify that the attached information has been provided by a specific trusted source. You want to be quite sure that a statement sent to your accounting program that you owe money to an online retailer is not a forgery generated by the computer-savvy teenager next door. Agents should be skeptical of assertions that they read on the Semantic Web until they have checked the sources of information. (We wish more *people* would learn to do this on the Web as it is!)

Many automated Web-based services already exist without semantics, but other programs such as agents have no way to locate one that will perform a specific function. This process, called service discovery, can happen only when there is a common language to describe a service in a way that lets other agents "understand" both the function offered and how to take advantage of it. Services and agents can advertise their function by, for example, depositing such descriptions in directories analogous to the Yellow Pages.

Some low-level service-discovery schemes are currently available, such as Microsoft's Universal Plug and Play, which focuses on connecting different types of devices, and Sun Microsystems's Jini, which aims to connect services. These initiatives, however, attack the problem at a structural or syntactic level and rely heavily on standardization of a predetermined set of functionality descriptions. Standardization can only go so far, because we can't anticipate all possible future needs.

The Semantic Web, in contrast, is more flexible. The consumer and producer agents can reach a shared understanding by exchanging ontologies, which provide the vocabulary needed for discussion. Agents can even "bootstrap" new reasoning capabilities when they discover new ontologies. Semantics also makes it easier to take advantage of a service that only partially matches a request.

A typical process will involve the creation of a "value chain" in which subassemblies of information are passed from one agent to another, each one "adding value," to construct the final product requested by the end user. Make no mistake: to create complicated value chains automatically on demand, some agents will exploit artificial-intelligence technologies in addition to the Semantic Web. But the Semantic Web will provide the foundations and the framework to make such technologies more feasible.

Putting all these features together results in the abilities exhibited by Pete's and Lucy's agents in the scenario that opened this article. Their agents would have delegated the task in piecemeal fashion to other services and agents discovered through service advertisements. For example, they could have used a *trusted* service to take a list of *providers* and determine which of them are *in-plan* for a specified *insurance plan* and *course of treatment*. The list of providers would have been supplied by another search service, et cetera. These activities formed chains in which a large amount of data distributed across the Web (and almost worthless in that form) was progressively reduced to the small amount of data of high value to Pete and Lucy—a plan of appointments to fit their schedules and other requirements.

In the next step, the Semantic Web will break out of the virtual realm and extend into our physical world. URIs can point to anything, including physical entities, which means we can use the RDF language to describe devices such as cell phones and TVs. Such devices can advertise their functionality—what they can do and how they are controlled—much like software agents. Being much more flexible than low-level schemes such as Universal Plug and Play, such a semantic approach opens up a world of exciting possibilities.

For instance, what today is called home automation requires careful configuration for appliances to work together. Semantic descriptions of device capabilities and functionality will let us achieve such automation with minimal human intervention. A trivial example occurs when Pete answers his phone and the stereo sound is turned down. Instead of having to program each specific appliance, he could program such a function once and for all to cover every *local* device that advertises having a *volume control*—the TV, the DVD player and even the media players on the laptop that he brought home from work this one evening.

The first concrete steps have already been taken in this area, with work on developing a standard for describing functional capabilities of devices (such as screen sizes) and user preferences. Built on RDF, this standard is called Composite Capability/Preference Profile (CC/PP). Initially it will let cell phones and other nonstandard Web clients describe their characteristics so that Web content can be tailored for them on the fly. Later, when we add the full versatility of languages for handling ontologies and logic, devices could automatically seek out and employ services and other devices for added information or functionality. It is not hard to imagine your Web-enabled microwave oven consulting the frozen-food manufacturer's Web site for optimal cooking parameters.

What is the Killer App?

AFTER WE GIVE a presentation about the Semantic Web, we're often asked, "Okay, so what is the killer application of the Semantic Web?" The "killer app" of any technology, of course, is the application that brings a user to investigate the technology and start using it. The transistor radio was a killer app of transistors, and the cell phone is a killer app of wireless technology.

So what do we answer? "The Semantic Web is the killer app."

At this point we're likely to be told we're crazy, so we ask a question in turn: "Well, what's the killer app of the World Wide Web?" Now we're being stared at kind of fish-eyed, so we answer ourselves: "The Web is the killer app of the Internet. The Semantic Web is another killer app of that magnitude."

The point here is that the abilities of the Semantic Web are too general to be thought about in terms of solving one key problem or creating one essential gizmo. It will have uses we haven't dreamed of.

Nevertheless, we can foresee some disarming (if not actually killer) apps that will drive initial use. Online catalogs with semantic markup will benefit both buyers and sellers. Electronic commerce transactions will be easier for small businesses to set up securely with greater autonomy. And one final example: you make reservations for an extended trip abroad. The airlines, hotels, soccer stadiums and so on return confirmations with semantic markup. All the schedules load directly into your date book and all the expenses directly into your accounting program, no matter what semantics-enabled software you use. No more laborious cutting and pasting from e-mail. No need for all the businesses to supply the data in half a dozen different formats or to create and impose their own standard format.

Evolution of Knowledge

THE SEMANTIC WEB is not "merely" the tool for conducting individual tasks that we have discussed so far. In addition, if properly designed, the Semantic Web can assist the evolution of human knowledge as a whole.

Human endeavor is caught in an eternal tension between the effectiveness of small groups acting independently and the need to mesh with the wider community. A small group can innovate rapidly and efficiently, but this produces a subculture whose concepts are not understood by others. Coordinating actions across a large group, however, is painfully slow and takes an enormous amount of communication. The world works across the spectrum between these extremes, with a tendency to start small—from the personal idea—and move toward a wider understanding over time.

An essential process is the joining together of subcultures when a wider common language is needed. Often two groups independently develop very similar concepts, and describing the relation between them brings great benefits. Like a Finnish-English dictionary, or a weights-and-measures conversion table, the relations allow communication and collaboration even when the commonality of concept has not (yet) led to a commonality of terms.

The Semantic Web, in naming every concept simply by a URI, lets anyone express new concepts that they invent with minimal effort. Its unifying logical language will enable these concepts to be progressively linked into a universal Web. This structure will open up the knowledge and workings of humankind to meaningful analysis by software agents, providing a new class of tools by which we can live, work and learn together.

The Authors

TIM BERNERS-LEE, JAMES HENDLER and *ORA LASSILA* are individually and collectively obsessed with the potential of Semantic Web technology. Berners-Lee is director of the World Wide Web Consortium (W3C) and a researcher at the Laboratory for Computer Science at the Massachusetts Institute of Technology. When he invented the Web in 1989, he intended it to carry more semantics than became common practice. Hendler is professor of computer science at the University of Maryland at College Park, where he has been doing research on knowledge representation in a Web context for a number of years. He and his graduate research group developed SHOE, the first Web-based knowledge representation language to demonstrate many of the agent capabilities described in this article. Hendler is also responsible for agent-based computing research at the Defense Advanced Research Projects Agency (DARPA) in Arlington, Va. Lassila is a research fellow at the Nokia Research Center in Boston, chief scientist of Nokia Venture Partners and a member of the W3C Advisory Board. Frustrated with the difficulty of building agents and automating tasks on the Web, he co-authored W3C's RDF specification, which serves as the foundation for many current Semantic Web efforts.

More to Explore

Weaving the Web: The Original Design and Ultimate Destiny of the World Wide Web by Its Inventor. Tim Berners-Lee, with Mark Fischetti. Harper San Francisco, 1999.

An enhanced version of this article is on the
Scientific American Web site, with additional
material and links.

World Wide Web Consortium (W3C): **www.w3.org/**

W3C Semantic Web Activity: **www.w3.org/2001/sw/**

An introduction to ontologies: **www.SemanticWeb.org/
knowmarkup.html**

*Simple HTML Ontology Extensions Frequently Asked
Questions* (SHOE FAQ): **www.cs.umd.edu/projects/
plus/SHOE/faq.html**

DARPA Agent Markup Language (DAML) home page:
www.daml.org/

"The Worldwide
7. Computer"

by David P. Anderson and John Kubiatowicz

An operating system spanning the Internet would bring the power of millions of the world's Internet-connected PCs to everyone's fingertips

When Mary gets home from work and goes to her PC to check e-mail, the PC isn't just sitting there. It's working for a biotech company, matching gene sequences to a library of protein molecules. Its DSL connection is busy downloading a block of radio telescope data to be analyzed later. Its disk contains, in addition to Mary's own files, encrypted fragments of thousands of other files. Occasionally one of these fragments is read and transmitted; it's part of a movie that someone is watching in Helsinki. Then Mary moves the mouse, and this activity abruptly stops. Now the PC and its network connection are all hers.

This sharing of resources doesn't stop at her desktop computer. The laptop computer in her satchel is turned off, but its disk is filled with bits and pieces of other people's files, as part of a distributed backup system. Mary's critical files are backed up in the same way, saved on dozens of disks around the world.

Later, Mary watches an independent film on her Internet-connected digital television, using a pay-per-view system. The movie is assembled on the fly from fragments on several hundred computers belonging to people like her.

Mary's computers are moonlighting for other people. But they're not giving anything away for free. As her PC works, pennies trickle into her virtual bank account. The payments come from the biotech company, the movie system and the backup service. Instead of buying expensive "server farms," these companies are renting time and space, not just on Mary's two computers but on millions of others as well. It's a win-win situation. The companies save money on hardware, which enables, for instance, the movie-viewing service to offer obscure movies. Mary earns a little cash, her files are backed up, and she gets to watch an indie film. All this could happen with an Internet-scale operating system (ISOS) to provide the necessary "glue" to link the processing and storage capabilities of millions of independent computers.

Internet-Scale Applications

ALTHOUGH MARY'S WORLD is fictional—and an Internet-scale operating system does not yet exist—developers have already produced a number of Internet-scale, or peer-to-peer, applications that attempt to tap the vast array of underutilized machines available through the Internet. These applications accomplish goals that would be difficult, unaffordable or impossible to attain using dedicated computers. Further, today's systems

COMPUTING

GIMPS (Great Internet Mersenne Prime Search): www.mersenne.org/
Searches for large prime numbers. About 130,000 people are signed up, and five new primes have been found, including the largest prime known, which has four million digits.

distributed.net: www.distributed.net/
Has decrypted several messages by using brute-force searches through the space of possible encryption keys. More than 100 billion keys are tried each second on its current decryption project. Also searches for sets of numbers called optimal Golomb rulers, which have applications in coding and communications.

SETI@home (Search for Extraterrestrial Intelligence):
http://setiathome.berkeley.edu/
Analyzes radio telescope data, searching for signals of extraterrestrial origin. A total of 3.4 million users have devoted more than 800,000 years of processor time to the task.

folding@home: http://folding.stanford.edu/
Run by Vijay Pande's group in the chemistry department at Stanford University, this project has about 20,000 computers performing molecular-dynamics simulations of how proteins fold, including the folding of Alzheimer amyloid-beta protein.

Intel/United Devices cancer research project:
http://members.ud.com/projects/cancer/
Searches for possible cancer drugs by testing which of 3.5 billion molecules are best shaped to bind to any one of eight proteins that cancers need to grow.

STORAGE

Napster: www.napster.com/
Allowed users to share digital music. A central database stored the locations of all files, but data were transferred directly between user systems. Songwriters and music publishers brought a class-action lawsuit against Napster. The parties reached an agreement whereby rights to the music would be licensed to Napster and artists would be paid, but the new fee-based service had not started as of January 2002.

Gnutella: www.gnutella.com/
Provides a private, secure shared file system. There is no central server; instead a request for a file is passed from each computer to all its neighbors.

Freenet: http://freenetproject.org/
Offers a similar service to Gnutella but uses a better file-location protocol. Designed to keep file requesters and suppliers anonymous and to make it difficult for a host owner to determine or be held responsible for the Freenet files stored on his computer.

Mojo Nation: www.mojonation.net/
Also similar to Gnutella, but files are broken into small pieces that are stored on different computers to improve the rate at which data can be uploaded to the network. A virtual payment system encourages users to provide resources.

Fasttrack P2P Stack: www.fasttrack.nu/
A peer-to-peer system in which more powerful computers become search hubs as needed. This software underlies the Grokster, MusicCity ("Morpheus") and KaZaA file-sharing services.

are just the beginning: we can easily conceive of archival services that could be relied on for hundreds of years and intelligent search engines for tomorrow's Semantic Web [see "The Semantic Web," by Tim Berners-Lee, James Hendler and Ora Lassila; SCIENTIFIC AMERICAN, May 2001].

Unfortunately, the creation of Internet-scale applications remains an imposing challenge. Developers must build each new application from the ground up, with much effort spent on technical matters, such as maintaining a database of users, that have little to do with the application itself. If Internet-scale applications are to become mainstream, these infrastructure issues must be dealt with once and for all.

We can gain inspiration for eliminating this duplicate effort from operating systems such as Unix and Microsoft Windows. An operating system provides a virtual computing environment in which programs operate as if they were in sole possession of the computer. It shields programmers from the painful details of memory and disk allocation, communication protocols, scheduling of myriad processes, and interfaces to devices for data input and output. An operating system greatly simplifies the development of new computer programs. Similarly, an Internet-scale operating system would simplify the development of new distributed applications.

An ISOS consists of a thin layer of software (an ISOS agent) that runs on each "host" computer (such as Mary's) and a central coordinating system that runs on one or more ISOS server complexes. This veneer of software would provide only the core functions of allocating and scheduling resources for each task, handling communication among host computers and determining the reimbursement required for each machine. This type of operating system, called a micro-kernel, relegates higher-level functions to programs that make use of the operating system but are not a part of it. For instance, Mary would not use the ISOS directly to save her files as pieces distributed across the Internet. She might run a backup application that used ISOS functions to do that for her. The ISOS would use principles borrowed from economics to apportion computing resources to different users efficiently and fairly and to compensate the owners of the resources.

Two broad types of applications might benefit from an ISOS. The first is distributed data processing, such as physical simulations, radio signal analysis, genetic analysis, computer graphics rendering and financial modeling. The second is distributed online services, such as file storage systems, databases, hosting of Web sites, streaming media (such as online video) and advanced Web search engines.

What's Mine Is Yours

COMPUTING TODAY operates predominantly as a private resource; organizations and individuals own the systems that they use. An ISOS would facilitate a new paradigm in which it would be routine to make use of resources all across the Internet. The resource pool—hosts able to compute or store data and networks able to transfer data between hosts—would still be individually owned, but they could work for anyone. Hosts would include desktops, laptops, server computers, network-attached storage devices and maybe handheld devices.

The Internet resource pool differs from private resource pools in several important ways. More than 150 million hosts are connected to the Internet, and the number is growing exponentially. Consequently, an ISOS could provide a virtual computer with potentially 150 million times the processing speed and storage capacity of a typical single computer. Even when this virtual computer is divided up among many users, and after one allows for the overhead of running the network, the result is a bigger, faster and cheaper computer than the users could own privately.

Moonlighting Computers

With Internet-scale applications, PCs around the world can work during times when they would otherwise sit idle. Here's how it works:

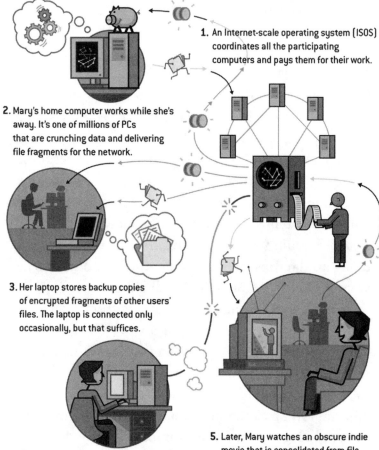

1. An Internet-scale operating system (ISOS) coordinates all the participating computers and pays them for their work.

2. Mary's home computer works while she's away. It's one of millions of PCs that are crunching data and delivering file fragments for the network.

3. Her laptop stores backup copies of encrypted fragments of other users' files. The laptop is connected only occasionally, but that suffices.

4. When Mary gets back on her PC, the work for the network is automatically suspended.

5. Later, Mary watches an obscure indie movie that is consolidated from file fragments delivered by the network.

Continual upgrading of the resource pool's hardware causes the total speed and capacity of this über-computer to increase even faster than the number of connected hosts. Also, the pool is self-maintaining: when a computer breaks down, its owner eventually fixes or replaces it.

Extraordinary parallel data transmission is possible with the Internet resource pool. Consider Mary's movie, being uploaded in fragments from perhaps 200 hosts. Each host may be a PC connected to the Internet by an antiquated 56k modem—far too slow to show a high-quality video—but combined they could deliver 10 megabits a second, better than a cable modem. Data stored in a distributed system are available from any location (with appropriate security safeguards) and can survive disasters that knock out sections of the resource pool. Great security is also possible, with systems that could not be compromised without breaking into, say, 10,000 computers.

In this way, the Internet-resource paradigm can increase the bounds of what is possible (such as higher speeds or larger data sets) for some applications, whereas for others it can lower the cost. For certain applications it may do neither—it's a paradigm, not a panacea. And designing an ISOS also presents a number of obstacles.

Some characteristics of the resource pool create difficulties that an ISOS must deal with. The resource pool is heterogeneous: Hosts have different processor

How a Distributed Service Would Work

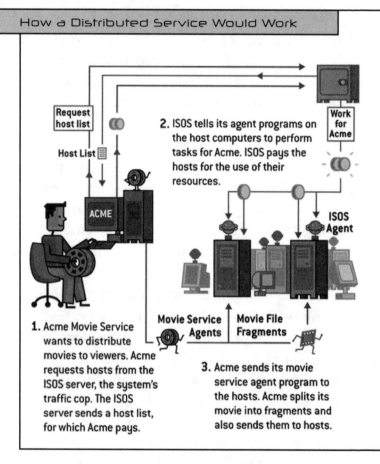

Request host list

Host List

ACME

2. ISOS tells its agent programs on the host computers to perform tasks for Acme. ISOS pays the hosts for the use of their resources.

Work for Acme

ISOS Agent

1. Acme Movie Service wants to distribute movies to viewers. Acme requests hosts from the ISOS server, the system's traffic cop. The ISOS server sends a host list, for which Acme pays.

Movie Service Agents | **Movie File Fragments**

3. Acme sends its movie service agent program to the hosts. Acme splits its movie into fragments and also sends them to hosts.

types and operating systems. They have varying amounts of memory and disk space and a wide range of Internet connection speeds. Some hosts are behind firewalls or other similar layers of software that prohibit or hinder incoming connections. Many hosts in the pool are available only sporadically; desktop PCs are turned off at night, and laptops and systems using modems are frequently not connected. Hosts disappear

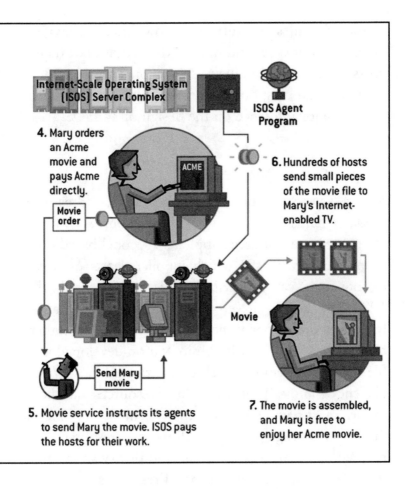

Internet-Scale Operating System (ISOS) Server Complex

ISOS Agent Program

4. Mary orders an Acme movie and pays Acme directly.

Movie order

6. Hundreds of hosts send small pieces of the movie file to Mary's Internet-enabled TV.

Movie

Send Mary movie

5. Movie service instructs its agents to send Mary the movie. ISOS pays the hosts for their work.

7. The movie is assembled, and Mary is free to enjoy her Acme movie.

unpredictably—sometimes permanently—and new hosts appear.

The ISOS must also take care not to antagonize the owners of hosts. It must have a minimal impact on the non-ISOS uses of the hosts, and it must respect limitations that owners may impose, such as allowing a host to be used only at night or only for specific types of applications. Yet the ISOS cannot trust every host to play by the rules in return for its own good behavior. Owners can inspect and modify the activities of their hosts. Curious and malicious users may attempt to disrupt, cheat or spoof the system. All these problems have a major influence on the design of an ISOS.

Who Gets What?

AN INTERNET-SCALE operating system must address two fundamental issues—how to allocate resources and how to compensate resource suppliers. A model based on economic principles in which suppliers lease resources to consumers can deal with both issues at once. In the 1980s researchers at Xerox PARC proposed and analyzed economic approaches to apportioning computer resources. More recently, Mojo Nation developed a file-sharing system in which users are paid in a virtual currency ("mojo") for use of their resources and they in turn must pay mojo to use the system. Such economic models encourage owners to allow their resources to be used by other organizations, and theory shows that they lead to optimal allocation of resources.

Even with 150 million hosts at its disposal, the ISOS will be dealing in "scarce" resources, because some tasks will request and be capable of using essentially unlimited resources. As it constantly decides where to run data-processing jobs and how to allocate storage space, the ISOS must try to perform tasks as cheaply as possible. It must also be fair, not allowing one task to run efficiently at the expense of another. Making these criteria precise—and devising scheduling algorithms to achieve them, even approximately—are areas of active research.

The economic system for a shared network must define the basic units of a resource, such as the use of a megabyte of disk space for a day, and assign values that take into account properties such as the rate, or bandwidth, at which the storage can be accessed and how frequently it is available to the network. The system must also define how resources are bought and sold (whether they are paid for in advance, for instance) and how prices are determined (by auction or by a price-setting middleman).

Within this framework, the ISOS must accurately and securely keep track of resource usage. The ISOS would have an internal bank with accounts for suppliers and consumers that it must credit or debit according to resource usage. Participants can convert between ISOS currency and real money. The ISOS must also ensure that any guarantees of resource availability can be met: Mary doesn't want her movie to grind to a halt partway through. The economic system lets resource suppliers control how their resources are used. For example, a PC owner might specify that her computer's processor can't be used between 9 A.M. and 5 P.M. unless a very high price is paid.

Money, of course, encourages fraud, and ISOS participants have many ways to try to defraud one another. For instance, resource sellers, by modifying or fooling the ISOS agent program running on their computer, may return fictitious results without doing any computation. Researchers have explored statistical methods for detecting malicious or malfunctioning hosts. A recent idea for preventing unearned computation credit is to ensure that each work unit has a number of intermediate results that the server can quickly check and that can be obtained only by performing the entire computation. Other approaches are needed to prevent fraud in data storage and service provision.

The cost of ISOS resources to end users will converge to a fraction of the cost of owning the hardware. Ideally, this fraction will be large enough to encourage owners to participate and small enough to make many Internet-scale applications economically feasible. A typical PC owner might see the system as a barter economy in which he gets free services, such as file backup and Web hosting, in exchange for the use of his otherwise idle processor time and disk space.

A Basic Architecture

WE ADVOCATE two basic principles in our ISOS design: a minimal core operating system and control by central servers. A computer operating system that provides only core functions is called a microkernel. Higher-level functions are built on top of it as user programs, allowing them to be debugged and replaced more easily. This approach was pioneered in academic research systems and has influenced some commercial systems, such as Windows NT. Most well-known operating systems, however, are not microkernels.

The core facilities of an ISOS include resource allocation (long-term assignment of hosts' processing power and storage), scheduling (putting jobs into queues, both across the system and within individual hosts), accounting of resource usage, and the basic mechanisms for distributing and executing application programs. The ISOS should not duplicate features of local operating systems running on hosts.

The system should be coordinated by servers operated by the ISOS provider, which could be a government-funded organization or a consortium of companies that are major resource sellers and buyers. (One can imagine competing ISOS providers, but we will keep things simple and assume a unique provider.) Centralization runs against the egalitarian approach popular in some peer-to-peer systems, but central servers are needed to ensure privacy of sensitive data, such as accounting data and other information about the resource hosts. Centralization might seem to require a control system that will become excessively large and unwieldy as the number of ISOS-connected hosts increases, and it appears to introduce a bottleneck that will choke the system anytime it is unavailable. These fears are unfounded: a reasonable number of servers can easily store information about every Internet-connected host and communicate with them regularly. Napster, for example, handled almost 60 million clients using a central server. Redundancy can be built into the server complex, and most ISOS online services can continue operating even with the servers temporarily unavailable.

Primes and Crimes

by Graham P. Collins

NO ONE HAS SEEN signs of extraterrestrials using a distributed computation project (yet), but people have found the largest-known prime numbers, five-figure reward money—and legal trouble.

The Great Internet Mersenne Prime Search (GIMPS), operating since 1996, has turned up five extremely large prime numbers so far. The fifth and largest was discovered in November 2001 by 20-year-old Michael Cameron of Owen Sound, Ontario. Mersenne primes can be expressed as $2^P - 1$, where P is itself a prime number. Cameron's is $2^{13,466,917} - 1$, which would take four million digits to write out. His computer spent 45 days discovering that his number is a prime; altogether the GIMPS network expended 13,000 years of computer time eliminating other numbers that could have been the 39th Mersenne.

The 38th Mersenne prime, a mere two million digits long, earned its discoverer (Nayan Hajratwala of Plymouth, Mich.) a $50,000 reward for being the first prime with more than a million digits. A prime with 10 million digits will win someone $100,000.

A Georgia computer technician, on the other hand, has found nothing but trouble through distributed computation. In 1999 David McOwen installed the client program for the "distributed.net" decryption project on computers in seven offices of the DeKalb Technical Institute, along with Y2K upgrades. During the Christmas holidays, the computers' activity was noticed, including small data uploads and downloads each day. In January 2000 McOwen was suspended, and he resigned soon thereafter.

Case closed? Case barely opened: The Georgia Bureau of Investigation spent 18 months investigating McOwen as a computer criminal, and in October 2001 he was charged with eight felonies under Georgia's computer crime law. The one count of computer theft and seven counts of computer trespass each carry a $50,000 fine and up to 15 years in prison. On January 17, a deal was announced whereby McOwen will serve one year of probation, pay $2,100 in restitution and perform 80 hours of community service unrelated to computers or technology.

Graham P. Collins is a staff writer and editor.

The ISOS server complex would maintain databases of resource descriptions, usage policies and task descriptions. The resource descriptions include, for example, the host's operating system, processor type and speed, total and free disk space, memory space, performance statistics of its network connections, and statistical descriptions of when it is powered on and connected to the network. Usage policies spell out the rules an owner has dictated for using her resources. Task descriptions include the resources assigned to an online service and the queued jobs of a data-processing task.

To make their computers available to the network, resource sellers contact the server complex (for instance, through a Web site) to download and install an ISOS agent program, to link resources to their ISOS account, and so on. The ISOS agent manages the host's resource usage. Periodically it obtains from the ISOS server complex a list of tasks to perform.

Resource buyers send the servers task requests and application agent programs (to be run on hosts). An online service provider can ask the ISOS for a set of hosts on which to run, specifying its resource requirements (for example, a distributed backup service could use sporadically connected resource hosts—Mary's laptop—which would cost less than constantly connected hosts). The ISOS supplies the service with addresses and descriptions of the granted hosts and allows the application agent program to communicate directly between hosts on which it is running. The service can request new hosts when some become unavailable. The ISOS does not dictate how clients make use of an online service, how the service responds or how clients are charged by the service (unlike the ISOS-controlled payments flowing from resource users to host owners).

What an Internet-Scale Operating System Could Do

By harnessing the massive unused computing resources of the global network, an ISOS would make short work of daunting number-crunching tasks and data storage. Here are just a few of the possibilities:

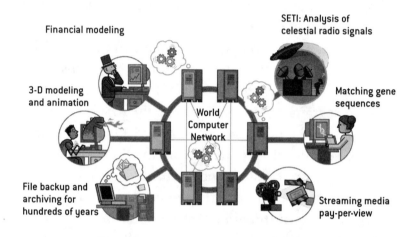

Financial modeling

SETI: Analysis of celestial radio signals

3-D modeling and animation

World Computer Network

Matching gene sequences

File backup and archiving for hundreds of years

Streaming media pay-per-view

An Application Toolkit

IN PRINCIPLE, the basic facilities of the ISOS—resource allocation, scheduling and communication—are sufficient to construct a wide variety of applications. Most applications, however, will have important subcomponents in common. It is useful, therefore, to have a software toolkit to further assist programmers in building new applications. Code for these facilities will be incorporated into applications on resource hosts. Examples of these facilities include:

Location independent routing. Applications running with the ISOS can spread copies of information and instances of computation among millions of resource hosts. They have to be able to access them again. To facilitate this, applications name objects under their purview with Globally Unique Identifiers (GUIDs). These names enable "location independent routing," which is the ability to send queries to objects without knowing their location. A simplistic approach to location independent routing could involve a database of GUIDs on a single machine, but that system is not amenable to handling queries from millions of hosts. Instead the ISOS toolkit distributes the database of GUIDs among resource hosts. This kind of distributed system is being explored in research projects such as the OceanStore persistent data storage project at the University of California at Berkeley.

Persistent data storage. Information stored by the ISOS must be able to survive a variety of mishaps. The persistent data facility aids in this task with mechanisms for encoding, reconstructing and repairing data. For maximum survivability, data are encoded with an "m-of-n" code. An m-of-n code is similar in principle to a hologram, from which a small piece suffices for reconstructing the whole image. The encoding spreads information over n fragments (on n resource hosts), any m of which are sufficient to reconstruct the data. For instance, the facility might encode a document into 64 fragments, any 16 of which suffice to reconstruct it. Continuous repair is also important. As fragments fail, the repair facility would regenerate them. If properly constructed, a persistent data facility could preserve information for hundreds of years.

Secure update. New problems arise when applications need to update stored information. For example, all copies of the information must be updated, and the object's GUID must point to its latest copy. An access control mechanism must prevent unauthorized persons from updating information. The secure update facility relies on Byzantine agreement protocols, in which a set of resource hosts come to a correct decision, even if a third of them are trying to lead the process astray.

Other facilities. The toolkit also assists by providing additional facilities, such as format conversion (to handle the heterogeneous nature of hosts) and synchronization libraries (to aid in cooperation among hosts).

An ISOS suffers from a familiar catch-22 that slows the adoption of many new technologies: Until a wide user base exists, only a limited set of applications will be feasible on the ISOS. Conversely, as long as the applications are few, the user base will remain small. But if a critical mass can be achieved by convincing enough developers and users of the intrinsic usefulness of an ISOS, the system should grow rapidly.

The Internet remains an immense untapped resource. The revolutionary rise in popularity of the World Wide Web has not changed that—it has made the resource pool all the larger. An Internet-scale operating system would free programmers to create applications that could run on this World Wide

Computer without worrying about the underlying hardware. Who knows what will result? Mary and her computers will be doing things we haven't even imagined.

The Authors

DAVID P. ANDERSON and *JOHN KUBIATOWICZ* are both associated with the University of California, Berkeley. Anderson was on the faculty of the computer science department from 1985 to 1991. He is now director of the SETI@home project and chief science officer of United Devices, a provider of distributed computing software that is allied with the distributed.net project. Kubiatowicz is an assistant professor of computer science at Berkeley and is chief architect of OceanStore, a distributed storage system under development with many of the properties required for an ISOS.

More to Explore

The Ecology of Computation. B. A. Huberman. North-Holland, 1988.

The Grid: Blueprint for a New Computing Infrastructure. Edited by Ian Foster and Carl Kesselman. Morgan Kaufmann Publishers, 1998.

Peer-to-Peer: Harnessing the Power of Disruptive Technologies. Edited by Andy Oram. O'Reilly & Associates, 2001.

Many research projects are working toward an
Internet-scale operating system, including:

Chord: **www.pdos.lcs.mit.edu/chord/**

Cosm: **www.mithral.com/projects/cosm/**

Eurogrid: **www.eurogrid.org/**

Farsite: **http://research.microsoft.com/sn/farsite/**

Grid Physics Network (Griphyn): **www.griphyn.org/**

OceanStore: **http://oceanstore.cs.berkeley.edu/**

Particle Physics Data Grid: **www.ppdg.net/**

Pastry: **www.research.microsoft.com/~antr/pastry/**

Tapestry: **www.cs.berkeley.edu/~ravenben/tapestry/**

Web Sites

Due to the changing nature of Internet links, Rosen
Publishing has developed an online list of Web sites
related to the subject of this book. This site is updated
regularly. Please use this link to access the list:

http://www.rosenlinks.com/saces/fuwe

For Further Reading

Battelle, John. *The Search: How Google and Its Rivals Rewrote the Rules of Business and Transformed Our Culture.* New York, NY: Penguin Group, 2005.

Daconta, Michael C., et al. *The Semantic Web: A Guide to the Future of XML, Web Services, and Knowledge Management.* Hoboken, NJ: John Wiley & Sons, Inc., 2003.

French, Laura. *Internet Pioneers: The Cyber-Elite* (Collective Biographies). Berkeley Heights, NJ: Enslow Publishers, Inc., 2001.

Head, Tom. *The Future of the Internet* (At Issue Series). Farmington Hills, MI: Greenhaven Press, 2005.

Richards, Sally. *FutureNet: The Past, Present, and Future of the Internet as Told by Its Creators and Visionaries.* Hoboken, NJ: John Wiley & Sons, Inc., 2002.

Index